LETTERS FROM A PEASANT

The Wit & Wisdom of a Prairie Farmer

By Brent Olson

Kirk House Publishers
Minneapolis, Minnesota

LETTERS FROM A PEASANT
The Wit & Wisdom of a Prairie Farmer

Photography courtesy of Brent Olson

Library of Congress Cataloging-in-Publication Data
Olson, Brent, 1954-
    Letters from a peasant : the wit and wisdom of a prairie farmer / by
Brent Olson.
        p.cm.
        ISBN 1-886513-43-0 (alk. paper)
    1. Minnesota—Social life and customs—Antecdotes. 2. Olson, Brent—
Anecdotes. Farmers—Minesota—Anecdotes. 4 Farm life-Minnesota—
Anecdotes. 5. Minnesota—Biography—Anecdotes. 6. Minnesota—Rural
conditions—Anecdotes. 7 Olson, Brent, 1954-Political and social views. I.
Title.
    F606.6.O47 2001
    977.6--dc21

                                                            20011029870

Kirk House Publishers, PO Box 390759, Minneapolis, MN 55439
Manufactured in the United States of America

Contents

Preface

Brent Olson, the peasant who has delivered these small essays into your hand, came to north Iceland recently with his wife Robin. He intended both to have a look at a new place – remarkably unlike western Minnesota where he practices daily life as a peasant, and to get some literary advice on yet another book he is planning to write. He faced an eight mile wide arctic fjord , with his back to steep craggy mountains. Most of the local peasants are sheep, horse or fish farmers, but I tracked down the location of a nearby pig farm and offered him the chance to go and have a look at it. Brent Olson declined – said he had quite enough of that at home, and had accumulated all the pig wisdom he needed for a while. He had mastered the craft of pigs.

He has also mastered the craft of the small genial essay in these sane and witty news dispatches from the daily life of a pig farmer. Olson calls himself as narrator – a "peasant," an old and unfashionable word from the days when the lord of the manor lazed about in his drawing room while the horny-handed laborers tended his pig sties, sheep cots, cow stalls, horse corrals. The master smelled of bay rum and sherry, the peasants of manure and sweat. Surely farming is not like that now? Surely Brent Olson is being disingenuous, ironic when he speaks into the voice of a "peasant" ?

Farming is, for better or worse, mostly a lost life for media-age Americans. It's hard to imagine a

New York investment banker or a Hollywood film agent as a Silicon Valley computer hacker making much of a connection between the food on his plate and the daily lives of fellow citizens. Is it possible for a pig farmer to think about spiritual or political life, family, history, economics, and bring useful wisdom to the rest of us who live outside the world of manure and sweat?

Brent Olson is a sneaky writer. He first charms us with his " aw-shucks, just a peasant on the prairies" tone, then after a little disquisition on, for example, long talky sermons in church, informs us that "the still small voice come of God is all around us, in a humming bird's flight, in a child´s tear, in an elderly lady's handshake. We just need to shut up and listen." These little essays are like dried tomatoes mysteriously hydrated. They keep expanding to be about the United States, the human condition, how to live a just life. They are much larger inside than three pages.

Before we turn our entire American countryside into a combination factory and theme park, we need to hear Brent Olson's voice, and the voices of many more "peasants" like him, bringing us news from the world of grass and pigs and long winters, sermons that go on too long and crops that sell for too little. As bacon is the essence of pork that has been first smoked and cured, then had the fat fried out of it till it is crisp and tasty, so has much of the cant and ignorance about rural life and real pig farming been melted out of these small essays. May readers enjoy the crisp and tasty result of Brent Olson´s wit and wisdom.

Bill Holm

Introduction

My desk faces east. It is a beautiful view. The sun is rising through the branches of the walnut tree my wife and I planted to honor the birth of our first daughter. It rises to the right of the barn my great-grandparents built and over the slough four generations of my family decided not to drain. I've lived in this house a quarter of a century and have seen this sunrise thousands of times. I never grow tired of it.

The view is not the reason the windows face the east. When my great-grandparents built this house, long before triple pane insulated windows, you planted trees on the north and west sides of your house and if you wanted a lot of windows, you faced them to the east and south, in effect keeping your back turned and your shoulders hunched to the fierce prevailing winds that blast this area of the country.

The sun is rising clear and red over the slough. It looks like the beginning of a beautiful day. In truth though, whether the sun rises clear or not isn't terribly important. What's important is what I can't see, the weather that comes sweeping across the prairie from the west and the north.

There should be some deep mystical significance to this, that I sit admiring the rising sun while turning my back on the harsh weather that may be coming.

But there isn't. It's what my people do.

I'm a peasant. We are the people who do the work of this world. We raise the food, cook the meals, and tend to the sick. There is no glory in being a peasant, but we are the ones who turn the wheels of the world, all the while waiting for the sunrise and all the while keeping our backs hunched against the cold north wind.

My father-in-law died this week. He and my wife's mother were married for 50 years. All this week she has moved in a sea of grief so profound that just watching her from the fringes has been the most exquisitely painful experience of my life. Through it all she has kept the dishes washed and the grandchildren hugged for she, too, is a peasant and her job is to keep moving, keep doing her best, though the wind may threaten to blow her over.

Watching Loretta and Bob's marriage all these years has been an example to me, and their daughter has been the best part of my life for a quarter of a century. I would like to thank them for that.

This book is dedicated to them.

Trouble with the Bishop

I once had a brief but very public tiff with a bishop and her cabinet. It wasn't a big deal,— timing more than anything else. I was at a big meeting, and they handed me an evaluation form to fill out five minutes after I'd sat through three of the dullest presentations since the invention of the overhead projector. I can say with complete certainty that I have never enjoyed myself in a room with an overhead projector.

On the first line of the evaluation I started out with, "Why are you wasting my time?" and then expanded on that theme for a couple of pages.

The moderator or facilitator or whatever he was called said that in the morning the first thing we would do would be to talk about what the evaluations had said.

The next morning I sat and squirmed in my seat. I didn't foresee a good ending here. Either they would make a big deal over my dissatisfaction, which would make me feel bad, or else they would ignore it, which would make me feel worse.

They ignored it and moved into the first topic of the day, entitled, "Listening to your customer."

That seemed like an unfortunate choice of topic.

I gathered myself, squared my shoulders, cleared my throat, stood up, and said, "Um, I'm not sure that you're listening to this customer."

A fairly spirited discussion followed.

After it was over, as good Methodists should, we adjourned for coffee. One of the innocent bystanders came up to me, put a friendly hand on my shoulder, and said, "When Daniel went into the lion's den, it was enough for him to just be there. He didn't need to pull their tails, too."

At the time, with my heart pounding from the stress of making a public spectacle of myself, I was inclined to agree with him. Over the years I've changed my mind. I've come to believe that the people in charge need to have their tails, if not tugged, certainly tweaked from time to time.

I read a book by Peggy Noonan a while ago entitled *What I Saw At The Revolution*. She was a speechwriter for Reagan and Bush, and in the book she explains that when she first came to work at the White House she was very intimidated by all the intelligent, accomplished people around her. After a few months she relaxed, because she had discovered she could hold her own. A few months after that her train of thought went something like, "Oh, no! We're the ones running the country?"

It's not just Republicans who think that way. An old story has Sam Rayburn telling a bemused Harry Truman not to worry, for the first six months he'd wonder how he got to Washington and after that he'd wonder how all those other jokers got there.

I think that's fairly accurate. Novels in which the plot involves some massive government conspiracy covering something up always amuse me. I am just completely unconvinced that any organization in this country, let alone the government, is well organized enough to cover anything up.

Brains are no guarantee of infallibility.

Brilliant minds worked around the clock for years to get us mired in Vietnam. Intelligent, experienced car people produced the Edsel, and *someone* in a position of authority developed microwaveable lutefisk.

So go ahead and pull tails. The people in charge don't always know what they're doing.

There is one small hitch. Tail pulling can be fun, and you may be tempted to do it more just for the entertainment value. Be careful about that. Excessive tail pulling can end all progress. If you pull something down, be prepared with an alternative to prop up in its place. As Sam Rayburn, the late, great Speaker of the House once said, "Any mule can kick down a barn. It takes a carpenter to build one."

Sometimes I look around and it seems as though we have a lot of mules. We need more carpenters.

This is what I do. Pull tails and tell tales. Telling tales come easily to me. After all, I've been a liar most of my life. Pulling tails takes a little more practice, but it's worth doing too. Because there are some tails just begging to be pulled.

Sometimes, This job is Just Too Easy

Sometimes this job is just too easy. I mean, I get paid to make fun of stuff that I think is stupid, and then I read in the paper an article about how much money the CEOs of large corporations make. What could be more fun than making fun of rich people?

Someone,—I'm guessing it's a guy with a mean streak who still feels bad because his momma put him through college while working for minimum wage,—developed an index that monitors how much more CEOs make compared to an average blue-collar worker. In 1999, the survey shows that the average big-company CEO makes *419 times as much money as the average worker.* Let me explain. I don't know how much money the average blue collar worker makes, so let's keep it conservative so as not to slander those good people who run the big companies. Suppose you're working in a fast food restaurant for about $7 an hour. That means the average CEO of a big company is making $2933.00 per hour. That'll flip your burger, if you know what I mean. I wonder if they get time and a half for overtime?

Rich people have an explanation for this. They say that a lot of this high pay is the result of stock options, which means that the higher a company's stock goes, the more money the boss makes. This is supposed to be a performance bonus—the better the company does, the better the boss does. That may well be true, but so what? The stock market has been going up like a rocket for years now. You could put a rabid chipmunk in charge of some of these companies and the stock would still go up. This is, of course, the American way. You get paid for what you do and the better you do, the more you make. After all, that is why Michael Jordan and Bill Gates make big money. They're better at what they do than anyone else. In these cases though, that doesn't hold water. There was a study done that showed in the past four years there has been a 19.2 percent annual return from the stocks in these large companies, while at the same time the boss's wages have gone up 39.1 percent *every year*. Okay, everyone out there whose wages have gone up 39 percent a year for the past four years, raise your hand. I imagine there aren't a lot of big shot CEOs who read this column, so I'm betting there aren't a lot of raised hands out there.

My favorite part of the article concerned Michael Eisner, the guy who runs Walt Disney. He made 595 million dollars last year. I know that seems like a lot of money, but 570 million of that was in stock options, so he actually only made 25 million dollars in straight wages.

I have two things to say about that. In my circle of acquaintances, a lot of people would consider 25 million dollars a year a fair living wage. And about the stock options—c'mon, Mike, do you really think you deserve a 570 million dollar bonus? I mean, Mahatma Gandhi probably should have made that kind of money, or perhaps Winston Churchill, or Martin Luther King Jr. And the year Michelangelo finished the Sistine Chapel I certainly hope there was a little something extra in his Christmas stocking. For most of the rest of us, that kind of bonus seems excessive.

Now, I'm not making fun of all rich people here. There are a lot of folks out there who had a good idea, worked night and day, risked everything they owned, had a little bit of luck, and ended up wealthy. To those people I say, congratulations, and I'll let you buy me lunch.

On the other hand, Mickey Mouse's boss worth 570 million dollars?!

You've gotta be kidding.

Dancing Pig

Some friends of mine in Lincoln, Nebraska, sent me a newspaper clipping. Evidently the Oscar Meyer Weinermobile was in town doing a promotion for hot dogs. The promotion was being held at the local zoo, with the idea being that a bunch of cute kids would show up to sing the hot dog jingle, "Oh I wish I were. . . ." It seemed to me to be a fairly harmless idea. The Weinermobile would sell a few hot dogs; the zoo would get a few more people visiting that day. All in all a win/win situation. Nothing controversial about a hot dog, that's for sure.

Boy, what a fool I am.

There were a few other people participating in the day's activities. They were there to protest the use of pork in hot dogs. One of the people was wearing a pink fuzzy pig suit and carrying a sign that said something like, "Pigs aren't food, they're friends!"

If I were a better person, I would pass on this cheap and easy subject. I'm sure these people are very serious and making fun of them won't help anything.

On the other hand, I get paid to make fun of people and this is too good to pass up.

First of all, I've spent almost 40 years of my life in fairly close proximity to hogs. They are not my friends. When we're having a party, I don't scout the hog barns in the morning looking for the most athletic pigs in case we need more players for the volleyball games. I don't go bowling with my pigs, and if we played cards together, I'm pretty sure they would cheat, if they didn't eat the cards first.

It's not just me either. When Lewis and Clark headed for the west coast, they didn't saddle up their trusty sow Ginger to show them the way. Lassie does not have a sidekick named Buffy the Berkshire. Even cats, which are the psychopaths of the animal world, are. . . more friendly than hogs.

Scientists say hogs are very smart. So what? Brains aren't all they're cracked up to be. Richard Nixon was smart as a whip, but I wouldn't have invited him over to play volleyball either. I don't have an opinion on how he would have tasted in a hot dog.

In case I haven't made myself clear, I think the person in the pink pig suit is nuts. And, there is a larger issue here. These people spent quite a bit of time and a significant amount of money protesting the Weinermobile. Signs aren't free, you know, and pink pig suits aren't either. Now, if this were just a hobby, I wouldn't say a word. In your spare time you can dress up like a pig, hang upside down from trees like a bat, or play golf wearing plaid shorts. It's none of my business. But these people don't do this as a hobby. It is more of a crusade, and they put themselves on a higher moral plane than the rest of us. That's where I differ from them. We live in a world that starves babies in the name of politics, slaughters innocents in the name of religion, and fouls the air and water in the name of profit. These are all problems that need to be addressed. I'm not saying we can solve them all, but we can make a start, maybe solve little bits and pieces of them.

After all the children are safe, fed, and educated, once we've started treating each other with dignity and respect no matter what our ethnic origin, once we've done what we can to stop screwing up the environment, maybe then we can dust off the pig suit.

Or maybe we can all just sit around a campfire, eating hot dogs and singing. ("Oh, I wish. . .")

Telling lies and insulting people isn't all I'm about. I do have a real job. I've been a farmer now for almost a quarter of a century. Farming has been an educational experience, in more ways than one. My education has been plenty expensive. Here are a few of the things I've learned.

I Like My Job

I like my job. There are a lot of days when I don't really realize it, but every now and then I remember.

We have been in the middle of a wet stretch here. We finished planting corn at the end of April and then it started to rain. We didn't get back in the field again until three weeks later. It was getting past time to get the soybeans in the ground, but I've been farming a long time now. I was a little nervous about the delay, but I wasn't frantic.

Okay, maybe I was a lot nervous.

Then the weather did what it almost always has

done. The skies cleared, the temperature rose, and the guy on TV said we'd probably have about a week of good weather before another wet front moved through.

We have a medium-sized farm, just my father and me working about 1200 acres. With a little over 600 acres of soybeans to plant, we thought a week would probably be about long enough for us to get the crop in the ground, if things went well and I didn't make any stupid decisions.

I started the week with a stupid decision. The first field we tried looked dry on top, but shortly after we pulled into it we just barely made it back to the road, with the tractor churning through the mud and the digger covered with soggy clay. I was climbing around on the digger, trying to clean it off a bit, when I slipped. My feet went out from under me and I fell directly on the frame.   I could have gotten badly hurt, but I cleverly broke my fall with my ribs. It was the first time in my life that I actually made the noise, "OOF." I sounded like the guy in a Batman cartoon who just got kicked in the stomach by Robin, the Boy Wonder.

I wasn't really hurt, but I couldn't stand up straight or breathe normally for about five days. This was, well, inconvenient.

We moved to a different field a few miles away. This one was drier and, we planted 140 acres in a day of sustained effort. More fields dried up, and we moved steadily across the ground, starting early and working late. The whole country was alive with machinery now, everyone rushing to get the crop in the ground. One morning around dawn I was in a field greasing machinery and I heard my neighbor start up his tractor from nearly a mile away. It was the first sound to break the stillness of the day. People who live where it's noisy have no idea how much you can hear when the world is just waking up. It was a morning of immense beauty. During my walk to the tractor I had disturbed two deer that bounded away. I was half done planting beans, working in a big field with no potholes or utility poles to contend with, and I had cheese curls in my lunch pail. Life was good.

We live in a world of noise, confusion, and doubt, and those occasional moments of clarity and focus are to be greatly appreciated.

We finished planting the beans and a day later received a nice little rain to restore the lost moisture and help sprout the beans. They're not up yet, although the wheat and corn are looking good. No one knows how the summer will turn out. I have a friend who is fond of saying, "Well, the day's early. Still plenty of time for things to go to hell." The weather, the markets, and the government all have the potential for causing disaster, but right now, today, there is the memory of a week's concentrated effort, a job well begun, and a chance for another year's crop.

And that's why I like my job.

The Importance of Self Delusion

I was singing "Born to be Wild" the other day while harvesting. That's a pretty picture isn't it? A chubby bald guy, inside a big dusty machine, driving up and down a bean field at two miles per hour singing, "Like a true nature's child, I was born, born to be wild!" At moments like that I always remember the words of a young woman we hired to take care of our kids one summer many years ago. She came out to the field to give me a message, and had to wait because I was at the far end of the field. The field was a half mile long and at, two or three miles per hour, it took me about 15 minutes to get back. She sat on the hood of her car and watched me the whole way. When I got close enough she ran across the stubble, climbed the ladder to the cab, and her first words were, "God! Is this boring or what!?"

I hate those occasional moments of clear thinking and sanity. It throws the rest of my life off badly. I've always been a believer in self-deception as the road to contentment.

I remember the last time I was embarrassed singing that song. It happened about ten years ago. For many years I would drive 300 miles into central Iowa and buy newborn baby pigs to be used for breeding stock. It doesn't matter why; you don't care and it would take way too long to explain. Suffice it to say that a couple of times a year I'd drive down one day and come back the next with a half-dozen very expensive little pigs. They were too little to ride in a regular trailer because they would get chilled. Over the years I tried several different techniques for hauling them with varying degrees of success.

One year I had just finished a grueling harvest season when it was time to make another trip. At that time, the vehicle I used for these ventures was a beat-up Chevy Chevette. It wasn't the sort of trip that anyone would actually look forward to. The pigs were very expensive, very fragile, and even though they were small, they were still pigs. They smelled terrible. And for those of you unfamiliar with the interior of a Chevette, there isn't a lot of spare air.

I was ready to go, though. I'd just finished a solid month of nothing but work, 14 to 18 hours a day, seven days a week. No time for anything but work and sleep, eating every single meal seated in the cab of a combine going up and down a field, and doing hog chores in the dark, either early in the morning or late at night.

I drove down to Iowa, checked into a motel, and spent the night sitting in front of the TV with my feet up and a bucket of chicken by my side. The novel sensation of doing absolutely nothing was a little disconcerting, but pleasant.

The next morning, feeling like a new man, I picked up my cargo and headed north.

Now, a dispassionate observer would have looked at me and said, "Hmm, there's a guy driving the cheapest car made in America through Iowa with what appears to be a back seat full of pigs. Poor bugger!"

Not from my point of view. I had my cap pulled down jauntily over my eyes, my toes were tapping, I was looking for adventure, and I was singing, "Born to be Wild."

I was almost back to Minnesota when I came to my senses and realized that there would be quite a few people who wouldn't consider this the ideal road trip.

Oh, well.

Reality is not all it's cracked up to be, and a little self-delusion is the fastest road to sustained sanity.

Headed West

We took a family vacation last week. Since we have this new daughter, a foreign exchange student, we thought we'd give her a real introduction to America, and we didn't fool around. We loaded the trunk of the car with sleeping bags, a tent, and other camping gear, loaded the front of the car with people, and headed for the Black Hills of South Dakota.

For those of you who don't know, the Black Hills are in the southwest corner of South Dakota. We live near the northeast corner of South Dakota. Now, the Black Hills is a terrific place to visit. The Black Hills, Mount Rushmore, Wall Drug, the Badlands, and Crazy Horse Mountain are all in a fairly compact area. The only downside to a vacation in the Black Hills is that you have to drive across South Dakota to get there.

It's not that I've got anything against South Dakota. It's a fine state. It's just that there's so much of it. We put 1200 miles on our car, we never left South Dakota, and—to be perfectly frank—a lot of the scenery is—well—a lot like the rest of the scenery.

We've a great videotape that our son and his best friend, Doug, made. The summer our son graduated from high school, he and Doug made a cross-country trip, taking along a video camera to record the highlights. The first 15 minutes of the tape shows a featureless landscape. Doug's voice, lowered and slowed down for dramatic emphasis, is saying, "Now, over this next hill you'll see the Black Hills of South Dakota." There would be more rolling pastureland and then Doug's voice would come back, "No, I guess not. Over this NEXT hill you'll see. . ." That went on for a while; then the tape stops because they got bored and put the camera away for the rest of the trip.

It sure gives you a measure of respect for the early settlers. I just about went insane and I was driving 70 miles per hour. I don't know what I would have done if I had been driving a wagon pulled by a couple oxen going 15 to 20 miles A DAY. And keep in mind, that was before there were any Wall Drug signs along the way for entertainment.

One of the first places we stopped when we reached the Badlands was an old homestead, made into a tourist attraction of sorts. The sod dugout was still there, a few falling-down buildings, and some chickens running around.

I've been a farmer way too long. As I looked around, my first thoughts were, "What in the world made these people think they could make a living here?" I mean, we're talking some rough country. We're talking about 20 acres to sustain one cow and that's when it rains. The people who own the homestead now are still farmers, but it takes 50 of these old 160-acre homesteads to support their family.

I have to admit, though, that the whole rundown, beat-up, gone-broke place gave me a feeling of pride. You see, this is where our country came from. This whole great big thing that we are all a part of came from places just like that homestead. It came from people who landed here with little or nothing; with just hard work, desperation, and a little luck, they made a tremendous country out of it. Granted, things don't always work out. A lot of these first farmers went broke, moved to town, or moved farther west and tried again. It's still happening. Success has never been easy, and sometimes it hasn't even been possible. Still, it's always been worth the effort.

See what a learning experience a vacation can be? And all this happened even before we made it to Wall Drug.

I love my job as a farmer. Of course, no one is just a job. I'm a husband and a father and a member of the community. A community that over the years has taken quite a few shots from people who reside in the "flashier" parts of the country. For instance, I recently met a woman whose total knowledge of rural America was based on "Green Acres" and "The Beverly Hillbillies."

Seriously.

She sang both theme songs to me, several times.

I don't mind living in an amusing section of the country, but on rare occasions I do get a little tired of my people being the butt of every joke. Now and then, I like to return the favor.

The Weak Ones

You know, almost every book I've read about people leaving the farm for the big city portrays the smart, sensitive, ambitious kid leaving, and the dumb, lazy ones staying behind.

This has always puzzled me a little bit. I live in the country, and I know some very smart, ambitious, talented people. I also know a fair number of incredible idiots, but that's the topic for another chapter.

It just dawned on me the other day that a reasonable explanation for this phenomenon, the smart-and-sensitive-ones-leave-the-country syndrome, is that these books I've read have all been written by the ones who left. Of course they think they are the smart ones, but there is another possibility.

A while ago we had a bunch of people out to our farm. It was a pleasant evening in June. The wind was out of the south so you couldn't smell the hog barns, our grove was shading us from the late afternoon sun, and, all in all, it was about the most pleasant spot on the face of the earth. I said to someone, "Can you imagine ever leaving a place like this?" Actually, I didn't say that. Someone else said it and I was standing nearby eavesdropping. I've found that, since I started writing my newspaper column, no one will talk to me for fear of ending up in the newspaper.

Granted, I've always felt that June on the prairie was a cruel trick. The flowers bloom, the crops grow, baby animals toddle around, and pretty soon you've forgotten about last winter. On the other hand, this really isn't a bad place to live. There's plenty of room, by and large neighbors do help each other out, and if there are flaws in the schools or churches, they're small enough so that it isn't impossible to fix them. So why are there so few people out here?

For one thing, it's a hard place to make a living. If you're a farmer, you work long hours, miss family reunions because the beans need to be sprayed, and never stop worrying about yields, prices, and overdue loans. I've done a lot of stuff in my life, from serving on any number of boards and committees to giving speeches on subjects I know nothing about, but I can safely say that the highest level of stress I've ever experienced comes from my daily task of farming. In the winter when there are no crops to raise there is marketing, planning for next year, doing your taxes, and convincing the banker you're good for another year. And that's if there isn't snow to move. There have been a couple winters where I haven't done much other than move massive piles of snow around my yard, depending on if I need to get to the grain bin or the hog house.

Of course, you don't have to be a farmer to live here. Most people aren't. That doesn't mean it's any easier. Wages tend to be lower than more populated areas. I know any number of couples who divide three or four jobs between them in order to make a living. If you own a business, you work very hard to sell your products to a diminishing number of customers while competing with the big stores in the big cities. In addition to working for money, most people work equally hard to keep the softball teams, the girl scouts, and the church committees going.

So here's my thought: Maybe all the people who write those books about the talented sensitive ones who leave the dull and drab countryside are the smart, ambitious, and sensitive ones.

Or maybe they're just the weak ones.

I've noticed that over the years I've become a little more introspective. As near as I can remember when I was 18 I had no actual thoughts—at least none that I can put down on paper. Since then, the longer I've been around, the more topics I see that really do deserve some thought. Of course, as a farmer, I spend most of my working hours alone. I'd like to think there are a few thoughts that pass through my head.

Hearts Desire

Something weird happened to me last week. Someone approached me about running for public office.

I really had to think about it. On one hand, I'm already getting paid for telling lies, so a move into politics might not be that big a move.

On the other hand, it would involve lots of meetings, being away from my family, and being nice to people I don't care for. These three things are nearly at the top of my don't-like-to-do list.

On the other hand (I know this makes three hands, but it was a complicated decision), I've always thought of myself as a put-my-money-where-my-mouth-is kind of guy. I've spent a lot of time complaining about politicians, so in all fairness perhaps I should try to walk a few miles in their shoes to see if I get bunions.

I have to tell you, I fretted about this a lot. I am, of course, a world-class worrier so fretting isn't a new thing to me, but even by my standards this was a tough call.

Job wise, I've always been lucky in that I've never really had to worry about whether people liked me or not. As a farmer and a writer, I can either do the job or I can't. Whether I'm charming doesn't matter. Politicians need to be likable. Well, except Jesse Helms.

For instance, every now and then we have a party at our house. Not every year, because sometimes it takes longer than a year to recover, but every now and then we have a party where we invite almost everyone we know to our house for the afternoon. Sometimes we even stop interesting looking strangers and invite them. We have people show up who weren't even invited, but know we would have invited them if we'd thought of it. It's that kind of a party.

So what if I went into politics and instead of inviting the people I wanted to invite, I started inviting the people I thought I should invite?

Well—ish.

There's an old saying, "Be careful what you wish for, you might just get it." What if instead of just complaining I was supposed to actually fix things?

There's another old saying that I think about even more. It goes, "The one thing you cannot trade for your heart's desire is your heart."

It seems to me that the people who rise to the top in any profession pay a very high price. Family, friends, peace of mind, all seem to suffer. I look at the two candidates for president and I'm sure they are both decent men, but over the years they have spent so much time running for office and saying the things that they think need to be said in order to get votes, I wonder if there is still something that they actually believe in any more. Are they still moved by ideas and ideals, or is it all just about winning?

There are so many arenas in life now where winning is the only thing. People are praised for being "willing to pay the price" and "single-minded." It's considered a good thing if someone is willing to work all hours, dedicating themselves to a job. "24/7" people say, meaning they're willing to work 24 hours a day, 7 days a week. It's the sort of thing politicians are supposed to do.

That's all well and good, but in a 24/7 lifestyle, how do you fit in parent/teacher conferences, teaching Sunday school, and family dinners where we compose new lyrics to the theme from "The Beverly Hillbillies"?

At this point in my life I like where I live, and I like what I do. I like my family, and I like the friends I already have. I'm not willing to trade any of it, even for a job that would probably be fascinating.

I'm just not willing to take a chance on trading my heart for my heart's desire.

Happy Fourth of July

I hope you have a good Fourth of July. It's one of those holidays, like Memorial Day, that seems to mean a little more to me every year. When I was a child, my overwhelming memory of the Fourth was my mom complaining as we sneaked back across the border from South Dakota with our illicit fireworks on the floor of the car. "All year long we teach our children to obey the law," she would say. "And then on the Fourth of July we show them how to break it." She never liked the smuggling, but she always did it.

Actually, now that I think about it, our way of celebrating the Fourth was profoundly American. We are not a very organized country. It is completely and totally in our national character to solemnly discuss, vote on and pass a law, then turn around and try to figure out a way to safely break it. It seems odd until you realize that we are a country settled entirely by people who left their homes because they thought they could do better. We are a country of the dispossessed, unsatisfied, and ambitious. We come from so many places, with so many different backgrounds, but all with the same dream. The dream is a simple one. We all came here just so that life could be a little better for our children, and we chanced everything on that hope.

As a country our diversity has always been our greatest weakness and our most profound strength. In the beginning the English didn't like the Dutch, and when the Germans came, no one liked them. Africans were forced here and rewarded by having everyone dislike them. The Irish came, fleeing for their lives from the great famine, and were greeted by signs saying, "No Irish Need Apply." Jews from all over Europe brought their own culture and were duly humiliated for it by people who'd gotten off the boat themselves just a few years earlier. Each succeeding wave of immigrants was thrust headlong into the melting pot, to sink or swim as best they could. Thomas Jefferson would have loved it. He worried that we would get too complacent as a country. "A little rebellion, now and then, is a good thing," he once said, "and as necessary in the political world as storms in the physical." We're still doing it. I lose track of who we're mad at now, the Asians or the Somalis, or whomever it is who got off the boat most recently. We'll work it out. We always do. We'll take the best and the worst from each new group and remake our country all over again. That's why the rest of the world makes fun of us, loves us, hates us. We're the big boys. As a country, we are trying to be sensitive bullies. We want everyone to like us while we do whatever we want, and the worst part is no one, least of all us, knows what that's going to be.

Of course, what the Fourth of July is supposed to be about is the Declaration of Independence. When you take a moment between the watermelon and the fireworks to think about the Declaration of Independence, I hope you'll think about the whole document. Pretty much everybody knows the "right to life, liberty, and the pursuit of happiness" part, but what a lot of people forget is, right at the end, where the founding fathers say, "We mutually pledge to each other our lives, our fortunes, and our sacred honor." As a nation of business people, we should all know that you don't get something for nothing. We've got freedom, but it hasn't been free. Another one of Thomas Jefferson's quotes is, "The tree of liberty must be refreshed from time to time with the blood of patriots and tyrants."

Definitely take a moment to think about that.

It's Hard to Get Right with God, When the Preacher Won't Shut Up.

I was talking to this guy the other day. He's a serious sort of fellow, and his religion is among the things he takes seriously. He leads a pretty high-stress sort of life and many times the pinnacle of his week is spending an hour Sunday morning sitting in a pew, listening to hymns, and getting right with God. There had been a few issues in his life that had come up recently, and he was really looking forward to Sunday morning so he could have a solid hour to think and sort things out.

He was telling me this as part of a story about the minister who had preached that day. He was a part-time preacher with full-time material saved up, and he gave the congregation both barrels. Not only a full-length sermon, but also lengthy interpretations of each Scripture lesson and even little comments on the hidden meanings of each hymn. It began to wear on this guy after a while, and by the end of the church service he was more frazzled than when he'd come in. He finished his story by saying, "It's hard to get right with God when the preacher won't shut up."

Can't argue with that.

Not being able to shut up is a common trait among humanity. When people are trying to prove a point, it seems that a lot of us figure that if one example is good, 17 examples, with little verbal footnotes and a bibliography after each one, are even better. It's a common problem among preachers also. You can't really blame them. They learn all this neat stuff in seminary, and after that they spend a lot more time studying and learning, and it is only natural that they would want to share it, all of it, with their congregations. And it is, after all, their job. It really isn't fair to criticize someone for doing something that by inclination, training, and job description comes naturally to him or her.

On the other hand, in I Kings 19, the Bible talks of Elijah going to a mountaintop to speak with God. There was a great wind, then an earthquake, and then a fire. God's voice was in none of these. After all the tumult was over there was heard the still, small voice of God.

My personal opinion is that the still, small voice of God is all around us—in a hummingbird's flight, in a child's tear, in an elderly lady's handshake.

We just need to shut up and listen.

Beauty

I saw the scariest thing on TV a while ago. It was an interview with the editor of some high-class women's magazine—*Cosmo* or *Vogue* or one of those.

Here was this lady, who looked to be of an age somewhere between 60 and moon rocks. She'd had so many face-lifts the corners of her mouth touched her earlobes. She weighed about 78 pounds and had an additional 15 pounds of make-up on. She was carrying an alligator purse, which seemed a fairly close match to her own skin.

Maybe it was her skin. I suppose the doctor would have to do something with the extra stuff he snipped off.

She was wearing some hideous concoction that looked like a feed sack with sequins and shoulder straps. In the interview she was giving an earnest talk on the necessity for style in a woman's life.

Could be she's right; I have nothing against style. She certainly doesn't have it.

I know, I'm being mean. It isn't nice to make fun of a lady who is old enough to be my mother and has spent that whole long life teetering around on stiletto heels.

On the other hand, she is the one who was holding herself up as an example of all that is gracious and elegant in American life.

I've got news for her. I am fairly heavily engaged in American life, and most of it doesn't look anything like her.

Don't get me wrong. If she wants to totter around, looking like an alien artifact from a sci-fi movie, I think she should go for it. It is no business of mine whatsoever. I just don't think she should be encouraging other people to imitate her.

Maybe I'm just jealous. In my life I have been called any number of things. To my knowledge, no one has ever called me stylish.

I'm not even really clear about what it is that constitutes style. I guess I always thought that you were stylish if your outward appearance helped clarify and enhance your inner beauty, showing to the best advantage your individuality. How can you possibly express your individuality when you get your fashion information from magazines that have nine pages of fashion tips and two hundred pages of advertisements for cosmetics? I also always thought that one of the prime requirements for a stylish person was self-confidence. How can you be self-confident if, before you go out in public, you have to transform yourself into some creature that in no way resembles what you really look like?

I realize I'm sounding a little grumpy here, but hey, I think the fashion Gestapo causes real damage. I mean, they are easy to make fun of. They wander around, wearing hideous clothes with hairdos that look like they got hit with an electric cattle prod, and they say stupid things like, "A girl can never be too rich or too thin." Well, news flash! There are some people on this planet who are too rich, because they've proved they don't know how to do anything useful with their money; and, when we have seven million women with eating disorders, yes, a girl can be too thin.

What's that line from that old country song? "Beauty is only skin deep, but ugly goes clear to the bone."

We've got plenty of ugly around, and some of it is considered stylish.

Tums

The other day I stopped at a convenience store and used all the money I had with me to buy a roll of Tums.

Is that symbolic or what?

I can't help but think that if I had enough money so I didn't need to scrape to buy a roll of Tums, I wouldn't need the Tums in the first place.

I read an interview a while ago given by some rich guy. I forget his name. Anyway, in the article he talked about all the pressure he was under, because he was worth several hundred million dollars. Any little shift in the stock market could cost him millions of dollars. He sure made it sound like having that much money was a burden hardly worth bearing, what with all the strain it put on him. He sounded pretty darn pitiful.

Sorry, I'm not buying it. The best rebuttal to that argument I ever heard was by Lee Trevino, the golfer. In case you don't know about him, he's a guy who grew up poor and somehow learned to golf. Golf isn't generally considered a poor boy's sport, but he got pretty good at it. For a while he even supported his family by hustling other golfers on the local course. After he got on the professional tour, in one of his first tournaments, he had to make a long putt in a playoff hole. Thousands of dollars were at stake. He made the putt, won the tournament, and when it was all over a reporter asked him how he stood the pressure. "Pressure?" he said. "There was no pressure. Pressure is playing for $5 a hole when you've only got $3 in your pocket."

I know a lot of people who pay their bills on Tuesday with the money they make on Monday. In fact, I know quite a few people who pay the bills on Thursday with the money they make on Friday, and if the paycheck doesn't show up until Saturday, things get a little tense. It is not a relaxing way to live. I'm betting that the per-capita expenditures on Tums are higher among the people I know than it is among the upper crust.

The experts say that the key to money management is long-range planning. That is sometimes easier said than done. The person who helps me with my taxes was looking over my books and commented on our personal spending for the year. It was higher than usual. I told him that our furnace quit and had to be replaced, our roof leaked and had to be shingled, and we wrecked our car and had to get another one. We didn't really plan on spending money on shingles, a furnace, and a car, but, what are you going to do? I suppose we could have trimmed expenses by moving out of our leaky, cold house. Of course, we would have had to walk to wherever we went.

I wonder what's going to happen this year?

I might need some more Tums. Care to share a roll?

I'm Going Backwards from Crazy

Did you see the movie, "Speed"? Not the new one with the cruise ship, but the first one, with the bus. In the end the hero catches the bad guy, who is holding a big sack full of ransom money. He is about to do something evil—the bad guy, that is—and the hero says, in a tone of disgust, "You're crazy." The bad guy holds up the big sack of money and says, "You're wrong, Jack. Poor people are crazy. Rich people are eccentric."

I've always wanted to be eccentric. The problem as I see it, is that not only am I not rich, I'm not even approaching rich. To be perfectly honest, I balanced my checkbook today, and it looks like I'm going backwards from crazy. I don't like to think where I'll end up.

I don't think about money all the time. I maybe dwell on it a little the first week of every month when all the bills come due, but there are entire days when I don't think about money at all. I realize that there are many things more important than money. In a lot of ways, I'm a pretty fortunate guy. I like my wife, I like my kids, and I even like my job, except for pumping pits. (Don't ask what that involves. Trust me, you don't want to know.) I live where I want to live, and by and large I do what I want to do. I probably live better than 95 percent of the people in the world. To some poor person from some poor country who lives on rice and maybe a boiled rat for Christmas, I'm a rich guy. I know all that.

Still, there are a few things that I might change. For instance, every now and then I look around the yard and plan where I would put the swimming pool. Not just an ordinary one, but one with a glass roof, heated all year round. Maybe with a couple of palm trees growing in the building with it. I'd put a waterfall on one end. Nothing too dramatic, just a little stream of water trickling over artistically placed rocks with moss imported from Japan growing on the rocks. Sometimes I think I would have a redwood hot tub in one corner, but lately I've been leaning towards just having a huge granite boulder hollowed out and polished instead. Maybe gold plated faucets would be a good touch. I imagine that would get a little spendy, but it sure would look nice. As long as I've decided to go with the granite hot tub, the whole pool area should probably be tiled with granite cobblestones. I think I should use granite because we once had a piece of marble in our kitchen and, when we spilled spaghetti sauce on it, it stained right away. I don't know if I'll be eating spaghetti in the pool, but there's no sense in not thinking ahead. I think the practical thing to do would be to put heat in the ground under the granite so that the floor would be warm to walk on all the time. There's nothing more uncomfortable than walking across a cold floor to get to your hot tub, don't you agree? I used to think that the glass roof should be clear, so I could float and look at the stars, but you know, it is cloudy a lot, so lately I've been thinking about having it made out of stained glass instead. Maybe a mural of famous pig farmers down through the ages would be tasteful.

I'm telling you, if I can ever make it back to crazy, I'm heading straight for eccentric.

Like Somebody

A while ago we had a large group of my daughter's friends at our house overnight. There was this school musical and, in the receiving line afterwards where everyone shakes all the actor's hands, we found out that there was going to be a cast party at our house. We smiled, exchanged the sort of look parents learn to use, and stopped at a convenience store for nachos and pop.

A lot of people panic at the thought of having a house full of teenagers, but I would rather entertain 30 teen-agers than I would six adults. Here's a little secret about teenagers. *They don't care if your house is clean.* They don't care if the drapes match the carpet, they don't care how much your dining room table cost, and they don't even care if the windows are washed. If the VCR works, if you don't complain about how loud the stereo is, and if there is plenty of food, you will make the little buggers perfectly content.

There was one girl in particular that I hadn't met before but of whom I became quite fond. A little while after the party, I sent the girl's parents a note congratulating them on having such a splendid child. I do stuff like that on occasion, probably not often enough. When I was 20, a friend of mine killed himself, and there has always been a lot I wish I could have told him. Since then, if I have a chance to say something good about someone, I try not to pass it up. It's kind of a big thing with me. I get fed up when people need to rush to the bedside of someone who's dying so they can tell them they are loved. The people I love, I try to keep them up to date on that so if a truck hits me I can just saunter towards the bright light without looking back.

Her parents sent back a short note thanking me, and at Christmas time I got a card from the girl telling me what a nice person I was. It's always pleasant to get mail like that, but the more I thought about it, the more it bothered me. You know why? *I hadn't done anything.* All I had done was like her. She was an eminently likable young woman. Some teenagers are on stage all the time, full of noise and energy and drawing attention to every thing they do. This girl wasn't like that at all. She was quiet, charming, and amusing. In a reasonable world she would travel through life in a cloud of approval and well wishes.

As we all know, we don't live in a reasonable world. I read a study not so long ago that tried to identify the common denominator between children who surmounted childhood and their ability to go on to lead successful lives. According to this study, the one thing that virtually all happy, successful people had in common was that when they were children, they all had at least one person who cared for them, who held them accountable and encouraged them. Liked them. Now I realize most young people have a lot more than one person who cares about them. I've gotten to know this young woman a little better now, and she seems to have just the family and friends you would hope for. I doubt if my letter meant anything more to her than a slight reinforcement of her knowledge that she is a valuable person. It certainly didn't do any harm. So get out there. Like somebody. I guarantee you won't regret it. You might even make a difference. It can't hurt.

Comet Problems

We saw a movie a while ago about a comet that was going to strike the earth and destroy all life on the surface. This sort of thing seems to happen fairly often in the movies, at least this year. I'm not very worried, because I've noticed that there are a lot of things that happen in movies that don't really happen very often in my world.

The government's plan to deal with the problem was to put two million people in great big caves for two years. After the dust had settled, these people were supposed to come out and start rebuilding civilization.

In the movie, the president is explaining on television why certain people were going to get to go into the caves. There would be a national lottery to choose some people, but by and large the lucky ones would be preselected according to their value to the world. The president listed off the categories of important people, namely scientists, doctors, and artists.

You know, throw some politicians and lawyers in there, and I'd rather stay outside and take my chances with the comet.

Let's look at this again. There you are, stuck in a cave for two years while outside all that is familiar has been destroyed. After two years the doors are cracked open and you venture out into a strange, bleak world to start over. Wouldn't you like to have a few guys along who know how to pour concrete? I mean, it's going to be a bit stuffy in those caves so I really think that people are going to want houses of their own pretty rapidly. For that matter how about some carpenters?

Food would be good, so I'd throw in some farmers and gardeners. Sure, there are lots of good gardening books out there, but like any other craft, you can't really learn how from a book. Trial and error will make you proficient after a while, but when two million people are standing in line holding their empty dinner plates, an oops in food production could be inconvenient.

We are trying to rebuild civilization here, so how about some teachers? I suppose the idea was that the scientists could double up as teachers, but I don't think that would work. They may be very smart people, but the ability to teach a six year old how to read is as much an art as a science, so I think we need some real teachers in there, too, not just folks with a lot of education.

Now in the movie, no one over the age of 50 was going to be allowed in the cave. That seems like a mistake. The first few years after the crash are going to be pretty bleak, with not very many frills, so I think you need to include some people who grew up poor during the Depression. They wouldn't pine away because there were no pizza places or cappuccino bars around. They'd just live on potato soup and pancakes and think things were swell.

They also could keep the other survivors humble with their stories of their own hard times. Can't you hear them? "Why, this is nothing. In '32, a comet twice as big as this one hit the earth, and we had to walk to school, barefoot, through a hail of flaming meteorites, up hill and against the wind. Appreciate what you've got and count your blessings; things could be a lot worse. Have another pancake."

Okay, maybe we wouldn't need a lot of the Depression survivors, but we should have a few.

Are the survivors going to rebuild civilization while walking everywhere? If not, maybe a mechanic or two would be handy.

If we needed to make room we could cut back on a few members of Congress.

Growing Up

Sometimes I am surprised that anyone actually makes it to maturity. At least anyone with older siblings.

I am speaking as the youngest of three children. No person who hasn't had an older brother or sister can know the torment we younger ones go through.

Well, maybe not. I know a lot of older brothers and sisters who are quite proud of the torment they put their kin through. They'll share their best tricks at the drop of a hat. I was just talking to a young woman who convinced her sister that the reason the little girl had an outie bellybutton was because, in order to keep her internal organs in adjustment, she had to give it a good hard tug every day. The sister told her that the rest of the family had been tugging the bellybutton since birth, but now she was old enough to take over the job herself.

The scam was discovered when the little girl woke up crying one day because she had forgotten to give her bellybutton a tug the day before and she figured a fatal internal organ disorder was going to happen any minute.

Okay. That is pretty funny, but what I want to know is, who's going to pay the therapy bill in 20 years?

Another woman I know well, really well (okay, she's my wife), was practicing giving her little sister a shampoo. She couldn't find any shampoo, so she used the next best thing, which happened to be canvas glue. She rubbed it in thoroughly, not raising much of a lather, and then tried to rinse it out. She started out rinsing gently, but the rinsing became progressively more panic-stricken as time went on.

You guessed it. They were calling her sister "Baldy" for most of the summer. She still favors short haircuts to this day. I don't know if she just got used to the look or if she's just trying not to give her sister any opportunities for further mischief.

I was fairly lucky in this regard. I did have two older sisters, but other than being faintly embarrassed that I was alive, I can't remember them being too hard on me. The worst thing they ever did was refusing to play Monopoly with me. Monopoly is a tough game to play by yourself and get any real satisfaction. My sisters are both a little bitter about my mother making them play with me. Both of them start to sneeze in an allergic reaction when they come close to a board game.

I never understood this until one of our kids got "Candyland" for a present. I played "Candyland" until I started to feel my brain shrink. The only thing that saved our family is that the dog ate most of the playing pieces and I accidentally broke the board over my knee one day.

I've seen studies that show you have the greatest chance of succeeding in life if you are an only child. I find that hard to believe. Sure, if there is only one child in the family they can afford to send that child to an expensive college, but on the other hand I can't think of a better way to hone your survival skills and sharpen your competitive instincts than to have a half dozen older brothers and sisters who are all trying to get a piece of white meat off a two pound chicken.

Mother's Day

It's Mother's Day this weekend.

I've got one, you know.

A mother, I mean.

The stories I could tell you about her! However, because she has threatened to disinherit me if I ever mention her in a column, I probably won't. On the other hand, if I could fit all the really funny stories about her in one column, it might be worth the risk.

No, I told her I wouldn't, and you really shouldn't lie to your mother.

But, if you should meet me on the street, feel free to ask me about the "sheepshank" story. If I don't put it in writing, she can't prove a thing.

I have been thinking about motherhood, though. It is a strange profession. No money, little glory, and guaranteed worries until the day you die. Babies are cute, at least most of them are, but that whole pregnancy thing looks like a lot of bother to me. And babies, even when they're cute, are incredibly demanding. And to tell the truth, taking care of them when they're babies is the easy part. Braces, Algebra II, and car insurance come to mind right off the top of my head. There's no pension and, truth be told, you never get to retire. There are little individual quirks among children that make motherhood even more interesting. When our son was very small, one week, ONE WEEK, after we wallpapered our living room he took a handful of

Vaseline and smeared it all over the wall. It was three years before we could afford new wallpaper.

Now that I think of it, babies are probably made cute by evolution as a survival tactic.

Still, most mothers I know don't seem to regret taking the plunge, so to speak.

I've been reading some of William Shakespeare's sonnets lately. (See, this is not only entertaining, it's educational as well. A fine value for the money.) Most of these sonnets are Shakespeare's attempts to get some woman to marry him. I am so glad that fashions have changed. If I would have had to write a sonnet to win my bride, I no doubt would be living all alone now, just a bitter bachelor eating Dinty Moore Beef Stew right out of the can. Anyway, in one of the sonnets, number 17 to be exact, Big Bill explains that this particular woman really should marry him and have children. The reason he gives is that he is writing all these sonnets bragging about her beauty and charm. Many years from now, he says, people will read these sonnets and think he was a liar, that no woman could be as wonderful as he is making her out to be. But, if she were to have children, then there would be proof. People could read the sonnets, then look at her children and see her beauty reflected twice, once in words and once in her children's faces

So, this Sunday tell your momma she's beautiful. If she won't believe you, tell her to take a close look at you. Your good looks had to come from someplace.

She's a mother. She'll believe you.

Father's Day

Well, here comes another Father's Day. I don't know much of the history of Father's Day. My understanding is that Mother's Day was invented to give flower shops something to do between Valentine's Day and Memorial Day, and then Father's Day came along to keep us from whining.

I may have a few details wrong, but I'm pretty sure Father's Day was just an afterthought.

Personally, I'm not too sure it's a good idea. Usually when I get special attention from my family, it isn't good news. For instance, "You're tracking mud!" "You're not going to wear that, are you?" and "Dad, about the car . . ."

You see? I would gladly give up my special place in the family during any one of those little scenarios.

Not that I'm knocking fatherhood. Granted, it is a lot more bother than I ever thought it would be, with no end in sight. And the job just seems to be getting more complicated. When your kids are little and they get the blues you can take them for a walk in the park, followed by some ice cream. Last winter when our son got the blues and would call from 10,000 miles away, there wasn't much we could do, except get sad ourselves.

All in all, though, I have to admit that fatherhood is the greatest thing that ever happened to me. It is difficult to imagine what my life would have been like without children, and it is impossible for me to describe what being a father feels like. So, since I can't think of the words, I'll steal some from someone else.

I get a lot of my philosophical insights from movies. Some people might think that makes me shallow. I just think it is a result of not getting out much. Anyway, a while back I saw the movie *The Man in the Iron Mask*. It takes place in France about 500 years ago. There are lots of swords, guys in cool clothes, horses galloping across the countryside—all sorts of things that have nothing to do with my daily life.

Near the end, a bad guy with a sword is assaulting the hero's son. The hero leaps between them and is stabbed by the sword meant to kill his son. As he is lying on the ground, dying, his son leans over him. The hero smiles up at the boy and says, "All of my life, this is how I wanted to die."

Now, I don't worry much about assassins carrying swords, but I know the feeling. A few years ago we had a terrible crop year. It was wet. Really wet. We struggled to put the crop in, struggled to get it sprayed and cultivated. Wheat harvest was a nightmare. I would walk around the field and convince myself that it was firm enough. I'd pull into the field with the combine and within five feet would be stuck tight. The harvest lasted for six weeks until the wheat had rotted in the field and the crop insurance adjuster told me to give up. When corn and bean harvest came around, they were worse. The crops weren't very good, and it was a constant, never-ending struggle to accomplish anything. We had to unload the combine on the road because the fields were too wet. After we put duals on the combine we could make a little progress, easily traced by the enormous ruts we left up and down the field. Harvest lasted for months. We tried getting up at 3:00 a.m. in hopes of enough frost to carry the equipment over the mud. We left our big tractor, with the towrope already attached, at the end of the field.

What made this more discouraging was that we knew there would be no chance for fall tillage and so we would head into the new year with the fields looking like a war had been fought over them.

Every morning I would sit in our empty kitchen, quite often to the sound of drizzle outside. I would eat some breakfast, take a long hard look at my work boots, breathe a deep sigh, put them on, and go out to work. The only thing, the ONLY thing, that made me put those boots on every morning, was that farming is the way I provide for my family, and you're not a farmer without a harvest. There were many mornings when a sword-wielding assassin would have been a welcome change.

Now, I don't want to get too dramatic here. There are a lot of fathers, any number of them probably, that have faced far greater challenges than I have. They cheerfully face these challenges, whether they require instinctive courage or gritty determination, for one reason. It's what fathers are supposed to do.

I know. I learned it from my father.

Getting Clean

For me, the hardest part about getting to church on time is getting clean first.

You see, I'm a hog farmer. One constant in my life is that every day of the year I have animals to take care of. Every Sunday morning I drag my tired old body out of bed and go through all the hog barns, feeding and checking to make sure all the animals are okay. Hopefully everyone else is showered and ready for church by the time I get back in the house. I have a beard so I don't need to shave, and I'm bald so I don't need to comb my hair. All I need to do to get ready is take a quick shower and hope my clean shirt isn't wrinkled. The problem is that I've awakened all the hogs on the farm, a thousand or more, and each one of them is trying to get a morning drink of water. By the time I climb in the shower, I'm lucky if there is an anemic little dribble coming out of the showerhead. It is a bother. I go through it every Sunday and, for the life of me, I can't think of a different way to do things.

It gets more complicated. My body isn't the only thing that needs cleaning up. We have three children, and I can remember many Sundays when by the time we got matching shoes on all of them, got everyone in the car, settled a couple fights on the way to church, we would stagger in halfway through the first hymn. I would settle into our pew, simmering with anger, and glare at my family. Now that they are older getting them ready for church on time is not the problem it once was, but there is still the occasional family dispute that can make the car feel very crowded.

On other Sundays I would bring the rest of the week into church with me, clinging to my clothes like a bad smell. I've sat in church and rehashed disputes with business partners, thought of things I should have told telemarketers, and worried about how next week's bills were going to get paid. Sometimes I'll find myself standing for the first hymn, moving my lips like I'm singing, but what I'm really thinking about is whether I remembered to get the oil changed in the pickup.

We all carry so much baggage with us, clinging to us like a bad smell. One of the chief functions of a Sunday morning church service is that we are supposed to have an opportunity to set that baggage down and rest for a bit.

Even when my thoughts stayed in church, for every time that I really listened to the sermon, there have been more times when I've noticed loose floor tile, cursed a bad sound system, and fretted about how the youth group was doing. By comparison, a paltry drizzle coming from my shower is no impediment to cleanliness at all.

You really should be clean when you walk into the church.

I just wish soap and water were enough.

Technically, You're a Creep

There are some goofy people in the world.

Goofy probably isn't the right word, but I'm pretty sure I'm not allowed to use the correct term.

Here's the story. One of the publications I write for has one of those electronic meeting rooms where people who don't know each other exchange messages. It's a little like sitting in a small town coffee shop exchanging stories, with one big difference. Since nobody knows anybody else, people are a little freer with their opinions than they would ordinarily be.

Anyway, a week or so ago a woman posted a message about some troubles that had just come upon her. It seems her daughter moved in with some guy. She got pregnant. The guy didn't want to marry her, didn't want any part of a baby, and told her to go get an abortion. The daughter didn't want an abortion and wouldn't leave the guy, so the prospective grandparents were thinking about adopting the baby themselves.

So far, this is just a sad story. Nothing new about it. Young women have been falling in love with worthless men for—how long—50,000 years? It's hard to know what to say to someone in a situation like that. You can offer your support, but the simple truth is that this is a tough spot with no simple solution. There could be a happy ending coming up, but it's a ways down the road.

I don't think the lady who posted the message was really looking for advice. I think she just needed to talk to someone and get a little sympathy. By and large, that's what she got.

Not from everyone, though.

Somebody posted a message saying that because the daughter wasn't married, this child-to-be wasn't a grandchild, it was technically a bastard.

Technically, buddy, you're a creep.

I mean, geez, what was the point of that? We live in a cold, hard world that regularly heaps pain and misery on poor souls who don't deserve any of it. Why take the time to add to the pile?

Sometimes it's okay to just shut up. Remember your momma telling you that if you couldn't say something nice you shouldn't say anything at all? There's really nothing wrong with that advice. Writing to a prospective grandma and calling her unborn grandchild names is just mean. It's pull-the-wings-off-butterflies mean and what makes it even nastier and low is that the guy was able to do it anonymously. Way to be tough, big fella. You used a fake name to insult an unborn child. What's next? Kicking puppies while wearing a Zorro mask?

If you're going to shoot off your mouth, you should at least use your real name and address.

We are talking about real people here. A father, a mother, a daughter, and a baby on the way. We live in a world that routinely does sickening, horrendous things to children. Some days just reading the headlines is almost more than a person can stand. And what makes it worse is that there is so much of this agony that we can do nothing about.

So, buddy, if you want to call somebody names, just drop me a line and get a load off your chest. It won't be the first time someone's yelled at me.

After all, if I pick on someone, I sign my name.

Don't Mind Me

True story. Really. I mean it.

I read an article about a religious cult in Texas that had predicted God would speak. Lots of cults say stuff like that, but these people nailed it down a little more. They said God would make an announcement on March 23, 1998. He was going to make this announcement on TV, channel 18 to be exact.

This would have been big news, but I'm sorry to say it didn't happen. To my knowledge God didn't say a thing on March 23, and I'm positive he didn't say anything on channel 18.

Actually, I'm not sorry it didn't happen. I pay attention to what is going on in the world, and it seems to me that the next time God does make an announcement it won't be good news, if you get my drift.

So far, it is just an amusing story. We have a lot of fruitcakes in our country (no offense, cult person), but what makes this a great story is what happened March 24. The leader of the cult called a press conference and said, "Well, I was wrong. I hope no one will listen to anything I say from now on."

What a chump. What kind of a leader is he, anyway? He makes a mistake, kind of a large one to be sure, but what does he do? A real leader would have blamed his staff, or said he'd been misquoted or misunderstood, or dropped on his head as a child.

No, he comes right out and says he was wrong and no one should listen to him anymore.

The guy has no future in politics, that's for sure.

Now, if this guy would have been watching television any time in the last 20 years, and not just channel 18, the Waiting for God Channel, he would have learned the way real leaders here in America act. When something good happens, the key is to leap to the front and take all the credit, whether you deserve it or not. That isn't so tough. Almost anyone can learn to do that. The hardest part is how to handle things when something bad happens. Then you have to master the ability to blame it all on your staff or blame the other party, or just say that what happened didn't really happen. Where do they teach this stuff? Well, they teach part of it in law school. Did you see that lawyer person on TV the other night, saying that there really is no such thing as the truth? According to him, the truth is different depending on who you are and which side you're on. Now, I realize it is a cheap shot to pick on lawyers. I mean, I know some lawyers whom I consider friends and they seem like decent enough folks, but every now and then their profession unleashes some real screwball ideas. Call me old fashioned, but I really think that there are some things that are right and some things that are clearly wrong. And when a person says or does something that puts them in the clearly wrong section, they should admit it, say they are sorry, and hopefully mean it. Not just sorry they got caught, but actually be sorry for the wrong thing they did.

That fruitcake in Texas can do it. Why do the people in charge have such trouble?

Harry Truman

I've been thinking about Harry Truman lately. You know, the former President. I'm not quite sure why he's been on my mind. It could be because this year is the 50th anniversary of his historic comeback victory in the 1948 presidential election. Then there's the whole Berlin airlift thing, when Harry gave the orders that saved Berlin from becoming Communist. He's always been one of my personal heroes so perhaps that's why he's on my mind. On the other hand, there is, of course, the novelty of a political leader who always said pretty much what he meant and actually did what he said he'd do. On top of that, maybe I like thinking about a president who fell in love with a young woman, courted her for years, married her when he got back from the war, and was a loyal faithful husband until the day he died.

You always knew just what Harry Truman was trying to say. He had one daughter. This daughter wanted a singing career. She got her musical talent from her father, who was a very good pianist himself. In fact, he used to say that when he was young, he had to choose between a life in politics or a career as the piano player in a whorehouse. He'd pause a moment then say, "Actually, there isn't much difference between the two."

Anyway, his daughter wanted to be a singer and was evidently pretty talented. However, after one performance a newspaper critic gave her a bad review. Harry may have been president, but he was also a father. He wrote the guy a letter that said, in part, "We've never met, but if we do, you'll need plenty of beefsteak for black eyes and perhaps a supporter below."

See what I mean? Nothing unclear about that message.

A lot of people know that he had a sign on his desk that said, "If you can't stand the heat, get out of the kitchen." What a lot of people don't know is that there was another sign that he thought about all the time. In a letter to his daughter he described a grave marker in the Boot Hill cemetery in Tombstone, Arizona. The marker says, "Here lies Jack Williams. He always done his damnedest." Harry thought that was about as fine an epitaph as a man could hope for.

Maybe that's the reason I've been thinking about Harry lately. Here I sit, looking at the markets. Today I could sell new crop corn for $1.35, beans for $4.44. I received a check in the mail for a load of butcher hogs. Good pigs, about eight tenths of an inch of backfat and about 54 percent lean. I netted $29 a hundredweight for the load. Not only is that not profitable, I'm not even sure I can see profitable from there.

I don't know how all this is going to work out. I don't even know for sure what I can do to combat low prices and lost markets. But I do know I'm going to do my damnedest to hang in there until things get better.

I hope you do, too.

Thanksgiving

Here we go folks. Time to stop whining and take a moment to examine exactly why you should spend a day being thankful. It is only one day, and there's food and football to fit in so you don't need to list every little thing, but you should be able to hit the highpoints. I'll go first.

First of all, my wife and children are all right. Wife and daughters are safely within arm's reach or at least in the same house as I, and our son is cradled gently in the bosom of the Marine Corps, currently at Camp Pendleton in California. Now, California is a long way away, but he spent last year's holidays floating around in the Persian Gulf waiting for some politician to do something stupid. (That has always struck me as one of the chief flaws in our world. When the old men in suits can't get along, the young people in uniform have to try and fix things at the risk of their lives.) Compared to last year, California is just fine.

Second, I'm feeling pretty good. Granted, I'm still losing hair and gaining weight, but as a friend of mine says, "Any day above dirt is a good one."

Third, I still like what I do. Once again, not a big item, but I know a lot of people who hate getting up in the morning. We had a very good crop this year. Yeah, I know, the prices are horrible, but I've had several years when I've gone into winter with nothing to sell. The fieldwork is done, but I have a mountain of bookwork and a lot of maintenance to do before I'm ready for next year. I don't handle boredom well and I don't have any hobbies, so it's a good thing that I know I'll have a full schedule every day when I open my eyes.

Fourth, I still like where I live. Western Minnesota doesn't make anyone's list of *Ten Most Scenic Spots*, but the slough is still open and full of geese. They keep the night alive with their chatter, calling back and forth, planning the trip south. The air here is still fresh and clear, the stars shine brightly at night, and everyone I pass on the road waves. As far as our state goes, we've elected a new governor, an ex-professional wrestler, and our football team is winning. The football team may bring us glory, and the new governor certainly should keep things interesting. On a larger scale, I'm still proud of my country. Not proud of everything you understand. Most days I'd just as soon the District of Columbia dropped into the Atlantic, but I've got news for the folks out there. The government is not the country. The America I know—and I know quite a bit of it—is still, by and large, kind and decent, hard working and friendly. We've got problems, hard, gut-wrenching, tough-to-solve problems, but we are still a going concern, no matter what the bozos on the Potomac are up to.

There's my list. Now you work on yours. Go ahead, give it a try. Stop whining. Be thankful.

At least for one day.

Butt in the Door

As a pig farmer, I've moved a lot of pigs from place to place. It always seems to follow the same basic scenario. I climb in a pen holding a gate. I open the door to the pen and then I start to herd the pigs towards the door. After a bit, there I am, at one end of the pen. There are a few panicky pigs racing around the pen, determined to never go through the door. The main group of pigs is clustered in front of the door, perfectly willing to go where I want them to go. And then, right in the middle of the doorway, one pig will stand with it's rear end completely blocking the exit. It isn't that this pig is opposed to going through the door. It's just completely oblivious to the fact that there is a door available. It stands there, lazily nosing around on the floor, with its big butt keeping any progress from being made. If you yell in frustration the pig might look at you with a "What?" expression on its face, but more likely it will not even look up, completely serene in the knowledge that it has done nothing wrong so the yelling couldn't possibly be directed at it. The truth, though, is that the panicky, not-through-the-door-at-any-price hogs really aren't a problem. They can be dealt with patiently after the bulk of the pigs are gone. The really serious impediment to getting the job done is the butt-in-the-door pigs.

In case you are wondering where this is leading, this particular insight came to me the other night while I was sitting in a meeting, wondering for the hundredth time if I could possibly fall asleep while at the same time giving the appearance of deep thought.

I don't know how many meetings I've suffered through in my life. Church meetings, co-op meetings, school meetings. I've helped plan town centennial celebrations and bake sales for the church youth group. Like most of you, if I wanted to I could go to a meeting of some sort every night. Of course, Lord knows why any rational person would want to. The one common thread among all those meetings over all these years is that the biggest problems don't come from the wild-eyed radicals, spewing ideas and enthusiasm all over the table, nor does it come from the moss-backed old tortoises who don't want to do anything new. The biggest obstacles to getting anything accomplished are the people sitting around the table with blank looks on their faces. You know the ones I mean. They get to the meeting early so they can have their pick of the free rolls. They take pride in always being a part of a unanimous vote. They can tell you how long they've been on the board, but can't really recall what they've accomplished. They're always ready to table a motion so they can think about if for a month, but then forget to do it. If you yell, they look at you with a blank, puzzled stare, much like, well much like a pig standing with his butt blocking the door.

I hope I haven't offended anyone.

Actually, that's not true. For Pete's sake, get your butt out of the way! We're trying to get something done here.

Yes, I mean you.

Pie Lady

I heard the greatest story the other day. It goes like this.

In some little town in Iowa there lived a lady who made the best pies. Everyone loved her pies and she took great pride in them, so every time there was a church festival or a school bake sale she would show up with armloads of her special pies. What made them so unique, other than their great taste, was that instead of little scallops around the edge of the crust, they had little tiny waves, about a quarter inch wide. People in the town would walk by a table full of pies and pick hers out just by those little waves on the edge of the crust. Sometimes people would ask her how she made those waves, but she would just smile and refuse to tell.

There was a church bake sale coming up, and some teenage boys without enough to do knew the lady would be making her pies and they decided to spy on her and find out her secret. They hid across the yard in the branches of a tree that overlooked the lady's kitchen window. She spent the morning working on her pies. First she made the fillings. It looked like she was going to make cherry pies, apple pies, and two blueberry pies. Once the fillings were made she set them aside and started to work on the piecrusts. She measured out the flour, lard, etc., for the piecrust, mixed it all up, then rolled it out. The boys were getting tired. They'd been in that tree a long time and the process of pie making is not that enthralling after a while. At last their patience was rewarded. The lady lined half a dozen pie plates with dough, smoothed the edges, looked around, and pulled her false teeth out of her mouth and rolled them around the edge of the crust, leaving a perfect series of little waves.

The boys didn't tell anyone. I'm not sure if they ever ate any more of her pie.

The whole story reminds me a little of the current brouhaha over our president. The people who keep track of that sort of thing say that all in all, he's done a pretty good job of being president. The stock market's gone up more than it's gone down, most people who want jobs have been able to find one, and at the moment we're not at war with anyone. All in all, not a bad pie you might say. But now we know everything that went into that pie and it's left many of us a little sick to our stomach. The pie's the same and so is the cook, but everything else is changed. We're all a little queasy, a little bit self-conscious. Some of us are angry with the cook for doing those disgusting things, and some of us are angry at those darn boys for telling us about it. And the only real question left is, are people still going to buy the pies?

God and Science

I always get a kick out of scientists who say they can prove that God does or does not exist. I get an equal kick out of the people in the religion business who talk about how they can prove that science does or does not prove the word of God.

Nothing personal here, but I think both groups are not only wrong, but they're also wasting their time and everyone else's.

Pay attention here, because you're about to hear the word of, well, the word of a small-town pig farmer whose formal training in these matters ended with Mr. Bakken's science class and Ted Colescott's confirmation class.

Did God create the heavens and earth? Yup. If we don't believe that, aren't we just wasting our time in church? Did it happen in six days? Probably not. I don't know and neither does anyone else. That's the thing about science. A few hundred years ago the finest minds in the world were certain the world was flat. Two hundred years ago the finest minds in America were equally convinced that anyone not white was inferior and women should never be allowed to vote. If I wasn't trying to keep this short, I could name a dozen more examples of very smart people being completely wrong.

This isn't some sort of anti-science diatribe here. Sure, theories change and new facts are discovered, making old theories look dumb. The curious, questioning, eternal search for the truth is probably the coolest thing about being a human being.

On the other hand, there is faith. You believe or you don't. If you need proof from some Ph.D. at Berkeley to have faith, then you really don't have anything, do you?

I may be one or two theories behind here, but isn't the current theory about the beginnings of the universe something along the lines of all the matter in the universe being condensed into one tiny area and then something happening that caused the cataclysmic explosion that started the whole ball rolling?

Sounds like a miracle to me.

I bet we could even fit "Let there be light" in there somewhere.

Where's My Thank You Note?

I read in the paper the other day that Cargill Inc. will report that it's third quarter earnings went up 53 percent this year over last year. In that three month period it appears that they made $192 million in profits. The article went on to state that the increased profits were due in large measure to the smaller prices paid to farmers.

Really? I never would have guessed.

I didn't get to see the whole report, just the article about it. I wonder if somewhere in it there was a thank-you note to all the farmers who made that profit possible?

Now, I have nothing against Cargill. I really don't. A guy I went to high school with works for them, and he seems nice enough. Unlike some businesses, Cargill certainly serves a useful purpose in the world. Someone has to buy the stuff I grow. I don't have time to go door to door in New York peddling corn flakes, flour, and pork chops, and I certainly don't have any desire to put on a three-piece suit and spend my life negotiating with the Chinese or Bulgarians about buying grain. I hope Cargill makes money. After all, it is a business and that's what businesses are supposed to do.

On the other hand, my farm is a business, too. A pretty darn important one from my point of view. Of course I have a family to support, but the money that passes through my hands also has an impact on our church, our school, and any number of local businesses. When I and guys like me make money, it ends up benefiting the whole country.

I wouldn't even have to make very much money. To tell you the truth, I don't have a lot of grand expectations from the markets nowadays. When I sell a load of hogs, it'd be nice if the check I received covered the costs involved, with a couple bucks left over. When I sell a load of grain it'd be really nice if the check would cover my farm payment, fertilizer and herbicide bills, with maybe a little extra for the bank.

It would be great to make enough money so the "chump" factor doesn't kick in. This winter I sold a load of hogs for 9.8 cents a pound. Then in a display of astonishingly bad timing on my part, I went to the grocery store and walked past the meat case where pork chops were $2.49 a pound. They were even on sale. I looked down to see if I had a "chump" sign on my chest, but there were none visible.

I didn't make a nasty public scene, but I certainly wanted to.

What makes this whole thing even more interesting is that Cargill does a lot of good in the world. The company provides food and agricultural supplies for large pieces of the planet. That's certainly a noble achievement. Cargill and the people who own it also contribute a lot of money to worthy causes and social advancement. In fact, I wouldn't be at all surprised if some of that $192 million in third quarter profits didn't end up being spent on counseling services and programs for desperate farm families.

That's really kind of funny when you think about it.

Actually, it isn't funny at all.

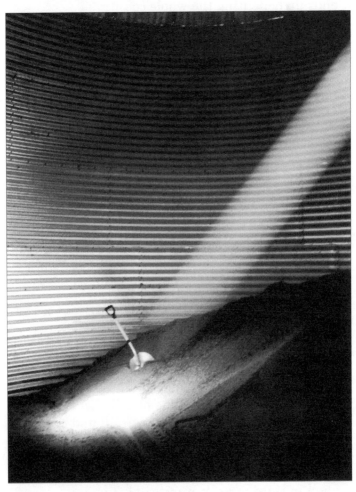

Anna's Roses

Anna's roses are blooming.

That's a big deal here at our house. No one would believe it, but on this whole farm the single most important plant is a scruffy yellow rose bush that sits in one corner of our yard.

It doesn't usually bloom this early. Ordinarily, the lilacs are in full bloom around Memorial Day, but we've had an unusual spring and the first yellow bud opened up about a week ago.

When we first moved to this place, 25 years ago, the rose bush consisted of one scrawny stem that was almost swallowed up by box elder sprouts and burdock. We hacked away the scrub brush and were rewarded by a few yellow blossoms. It's a good thing we knew nothing about landscaping and were completely broke besides, because no landscape designer in his right mind would have kept that pathetic little bush. With a little money to spend on new shrubs or even a little spare time to plant grass, we probably would have dug that thing up and thrown it away. It was almost destroyed by accident. Someone, who shall remain nameless, was burning leaves and the fire got out of control.

At first I didn't know it was Anna's rose bush. If I had, I would have saved it no matter how ugly it was.

Anna Elvabakke was a wonderful human being. I need to get that said right up front. She came to this country as a young woman and spent her life taking care of other people's families. She kept in contact with her family in Norway, but never saw them again. At one time in her life she had saved up enough money from her modest wages to return home, but the farmer she was working for was in danger of losing his farm. She gave him her savings so he could get a crop planted. The crop failed and he ended up losing his farm anyway, along with all of Anna's money.

When I was growing up, Anna was my Uncle Carl's housekeeper. We lived about a mile away and whenever life treated me badly, I would ride my bicycle to visit Anna. She would sit me at her kitchen table, feed me cookies, and tell me I was wonderful. Despite the fact that she was a maiden lady who never had children, she'd raised several for other people and she taught me most of what I needed to know about child rearing.

I'm not the only person who treasured her company. To this day I run into people whose lives were touched by her quiet kindness. I've lost track of the number of children who sat at her table, were fed cookies and nodded in agreement at being told they were wonderful.

It's funny, but if you looked at Anna's resumé you wouldn't be impressed. Her world was one long boat trip as a scared teenager, and the kitchens and gardens of a succession of small midwestern farms. No husband, no children, and when she passed away her possessions were reduced to photographs and letters on the wall of the small room in a local nursing home where she finished her days.

Her legacy? Hard to tell. She liked to keep busy and spent many hours crocheting lace and giving it away to anyone who stopped by. Doesn't seem like much, but there are lace-edged pillowcases all around the world, treasured by people who, when they were very small, sat in Anna's kitchen and listened to a gentle voice with a soft Norwegian accent telling them they were wonderful.

There are five cemeteries we visit on Memorial Day. One of them contains Anna's grave. Every year there are flowers on her grave, quite often from several different sources.

This year there will be yellow roses.

Looking for Stars on a Rainy Night

I lay on my back in the middle of the lawn, looking for stars. I'm not a big stargazer, but I couldn't stand to be in the house any more. It felt constrictive, and the company of other people was not what I wanted just then.

We had spent several hours that afternoon in the apartment of my son's best friend, Doug. Doug had been a part of our household since he was ten, and it was always a joy to visit with him. Charming, funny, and a great practical joker Doug also had an impressive gentleness of spirit. The people who ran the school system loved him, because he had a way of gathering in the strays that are found in any school and making them part of his group. He was a very nice kid.

He was also gravely ill with cancer.

He'd been struggling with cancer for two and a half years. From the beginning he had established rules we all had to abide by. No one was allowed to be down or maudlin around him, and he made few compromises with the disease. After my son graduated from high school he and Doug took our car on a tour of the western half of the country. Starting in Minnesota they drove to California, up along the coast, and back through the northern tier of states. Timing was critical because Doug only had two weeks between chemotherapy treatments. A broken clutch cable stalled them in Spokane for three days, and they drove from Spokane back to western Minnesota in twenty and a half hours. He had his trip, and he was on time for his appointment.

Doug was adamant about his rules so that afternoon we laughed and joked, told stories and teased.

Then my wife and I cried all the way home.

As I was lying on my back in the darkness trying to find stars in the unseen sky, it started to rain. The symbolism was, literally, almost more than I could bear.

In a reasonable world there would have been a short storm and then the skies would have cleared and the stars would have shone down in all their glory. In a reasonable world Doug's cancer would have been cured and he could have gotten on with his young life.

We don't live in a world that is anywhere close to being reasonable. I soon became uncomfortable in the soft drizzle and went into the house and rejoined my family.

Doug died a week later.

I had known, that evening, what was coming. I lay on my back and the raindrops mingled with my tears as my heart broke. I never did see the stars that night. The clouds were just too thick.

But I knew the stars were there.

I know they are there.

In my weekly columns I usually try to be a thoughtful guy, pointing out a few of the little things that might make you go "Hmmm."
On the other hand, sometimes I'm just a liar.

Why Men Look Better Than Women

Conversational tip: When you are talking to a woman who just got a new hairstyle, saying, "Is that how it's supposed to look?" is not your best choice. "Were you surprised when you looked in the mirror?" is also a phrase you might want to avoid.

I've been wondering why men think they look better than women. If you ever spend time in a mall, say, waiting for someone else to finish shopping, watch the people walking by. Some of the storefronts are just big mirrors. Usually women will walk right by the mirrors without looking. If they do look, they will quite often frown a little and adjust their hair or their skirt, give a little head shake, like, I am sooo ugly, then walk on. Next, you'll see some guy in plaid Bermuda shorts and a Daffy Duck T-shirt wearing black socks with sneakers go by the same mirror. He'll slow down, suck in his stomach, flex his flabby biceps, and give himself a big cheesy grin. He'll saunter off down the corridor, convinced again that he is in fact studly, a manly man, a chick magnet.

What makes this even more inexplicable is that women almost always look better than men do. There are exceptions. New mothers with babies that spit up on them come to mind immediately, but by and large, the average woman almost always looks better than the average man. You can't convince them of that, though. I don't think I have ever seen a woman look at herself in a full-length mirror, appraising herself from toe to top of head, then smile, give herself a big thumbs-up and say, "Stand back world. I'm looking good tonight!"

Not only do they look better, they work harder at looking better. I've got a suit in case someone gets married, I've got work clothes that are mainly stained and full of holes, and in between I've got a pair of blue jeans and about three shirts. Very few women can get by with a wardrobe that small. You know why? *They care what they look like.* And it isn't just clothes. Women wash their hair a lot and do stuff to it that takes a long time. It all looks like a lot of bother, even painful. Have you ever seen an eyelash curler? It looks like something the Spanish Inquisition used for plucking out eyeballs. No man would use one of those.

So why is it that after all that effort and all those implements and despite the fact that women are intrinsically more attractive than men, the dorkiest looking guy at the mall, complete with nose hair and bald spot, can convince himself that he is the answer to a maiden's prayers, while the impeccably groomed, perfectly dressed, intelligent, accomplished young woman ahead of him will avert her eyes when she passes a mirror, as though she was walking by a cage of snakes?

Life is a mystery sometimes.

Car Shopping

We've been car shopping lately. When we stopped at the first car lot, I pointed out a car that I felt was in the proper price range. My wife, being temporarily on crutches, asked me to go check out the interior. I looked carefully, then came back to the pickup.

"Yup," I said, "It's got one. Should I find a salesman and tell him we'll take it?"

She sighed and gave me a look. I've gotten a lot of those over the years and I've come to call it a wife look, although recently my children seem to have picked it up. I'm not sure what it means, but I do know it implies some level of frustration.

She said, "Maybe we should look just a little more."

I sighed.

I don't like car shopping. In fact, the only reason I would enjoy buying a car is because it would mean we wouldn't have to look for another one for four or five years. My wife doesn't like it either, and we've found we have to do it together. We've each done it alone, and the end result has not been satisfactory. We seem to have skills in car buying that complement each other.

I truly don't care about cars. If it has four wheels and a key, I'm happy. If it starts in the wintertime and the upholstery doesn't show stains, it's the perfect vehicle as far as I'm concerned. Since I am so oblivious to the finer points of any particular car, I am very good at projecting the correct air of indifference calculated to make a salesperson give us the lowest price. My attitude has always been that they make a million of these a day and if I can't afford this one, another one will do just as well. The last vehicle we had that I liked was a '66 Chevy pickup.

My wife, on the other hand, has some traits I'm lacking. For instance, an appreciation for style and practicality, not to mention airbags and air-conditioning. We truly do make a pretty good team, but it is not a comfortable experience. In fact, it is a little like wallpapering. A good marriage can survive it, but it isn't the sort of thing that should be put to the test very often.

We've done fairly well for years following this system but our latest car was wrecked only six months after we purchased it, long before the scars of the purchasing process had healed over.

Our first mistake was taking our daughters along. There are four of us who travel by car, but we spent a lot of time looking at Corvette convertibles. Not only are they out of our price range by several digits, but really, how well will they go through snowdrifts and how many sacks of feed will fit in the trunk? Another problem is that the prices are usually in little tiny letters or else you have to get a salesperson to tell you the price. This is wrong, because it gives you a chance to fall in love with an entirely unsuitable car. What is needed are price tags about four feet square. When you see a price you can afford, then you can lift up the tag and see if you like the car. It was exhausting driving around, having a member of the family say, "Oh look, I like that one," only to find that the price was more than the value of our home.

We did find a car.

We are still married.

We may not even drive it, just leave it safely in the garage, because if we have to buy another car anytime soon, things could get ugly.

Chocolate Chip Cookie Dough

Gee, I've had a hard week. Our church youth group was selling food at a local festival, and my wife and daughter decided to make monster cookies as our contribution. These are huge, plate filling chocolate chip cookies. They had no idea how many they would sell, so they made two recipes. How much cookie dough is that? I'll give you a hint. A single recipe calls for eighteen cups of oatmeal and two pounds of chocolate chips. They baked one batch and decided to wait and see how the cookies were selling before they baked the other batch.

The cookies didn't sell very well. The fruit cups sold well, and the barbecued pork sold out. Even the chocolate covered frozen bananas moved pretty well, but no one was in the market for giant chocolate chip cookies. Consumers are so fickle.

Here's the problem. They had cookies left over and didn't even need to bake the other batch.

We have about a bushel basket full of cookie dough in our refrigerator.

This is a bad thing. I've a confession to make. I am a cookie dough junkie. I've been getting my knuckles smacked for stealing cookie dough ever since I was four. My wife took over smoothly for my mother, and now my daughters have started whacking me every time I come into the kitchen when they're cooking. It is well worth the pain though. Nothing better than chocolate chip cookie dough.

You'd think that I'd be in seventh heaven, but it's too much. It's like a drunk winning a liquor store in the lottery, it's like a gambler being locked in a casino for a week, it's like a politician being asked to address a fundraising dinner sponsored by The Association of People With Way Too Much Money. I can't stand the pressure.

To top it off, I've been trying to lose weight. I have no choice; it's either drop a few pounds or buy new clothes. I'd been having a certain amount of success, but now, now when I come down for breakfast I have to LIFT THE GIGANTIC BOWL OF COOKIE DOUGH OUT OF THE WAY BEFORE I CAN GET TO THE LOWFAT YOGOURT! Lord, help me, I don't have that much willpower. I'm not sure I would want that much willpower.

Maybe there is no problem. Maybe this cookie dough is not really bad for me. Sure, it does have two pounds of brown sugar in it and all those chocolate chips. In addition there is a pound of M&Ms and about a dozen eggs, but how about that oatmeal? That should count for something shouldn't it? Plus, think of the time saving. If I have a regular breakfast I make a pot of coffee, sit down at the table, read for a while, maybe find something so interesting to read that I don't get out to work on time. This way I just grab a handful of dough and run out the door before anyone sees me.

My jeans do feel a bit snug this morning. Oatmeal is so bulky.

Interesting Life

I don't want to make the rest of you feel cheated, but I gotta tell you, I lead a fascinating life. And I don't even try.

I've spent the past three days as a chaperone on a band and choir trip. Just a half dozen other adults and me, along with 90 teenagers. I'd like to tell you all about it, but since I've only had six hours of sleep in three days, I'm just going to give you a couple highlights before I go to bed. Before I start, I would like to mention that in nearly a quarter of a century of working with young people, this was probably the most well-behaved group with whom I've ever traveled.

The first night I went along with about 20 kids on an optional trip to a dinner theatre. Dinner went just fine, but there was a slight hitch at dessert time. The waitress, who brought out an armload of desserts for one table of students, was also carrying a birthday cake for a person at another table.

This person was a complete stranger to all of us. That's an important part of the story, so remember it.

All of our students got up and followed the waitress. For a moment I thought they were planning to mug her and steal the cake, but instead they just surrounded the birthday stranger and, after asking his name, sang "Happy Birthday" to him, including a nifty bit of harmony. After receiving a nice round of applause from the rest of customers, the singers sat back down and finished their dinner.

The next night was a lot more interesting. When we had checked into our hotel, the tour leader told how just a year ago a tour group of high school students had stayed at this hotel. One member of the group had hung his clothes from a sprinkler head, tripped the alarm system, and flooded 14 rooms. The lawsuit had just been settled.

At about 1:00 a.m. the fire alarm went off in the hotel. I'm ashamed to say my first thought was, "I'm going to kill him/her." I walked out into a hall full of students and complete strangers milling about in their pajamas. Lights were flashing, the alarm was sounding, and there were several grim-faced chaperones stalking the corridor. I looked up and saw water dripping out of one of the smoke detectors. It looked bad, but then I remembered that we were on the top floor of the hotel   you have no idea how comforted I was by this. Sure, I was on the top floor of what might be a burning hotel with a bunch of kids, two of whom were my own, but whatever catastrophe was about the happen hadn't been caused by us.

We herded everyone downstairs and outside until the fire trucks came and several firemen agreed with us that rainwater dripping through a leaky roof and into a smoke detector could quite possibly make it go off. We got everyone back in bed. About ten minutes later the alarm went off again. It bleated a couple of times, then stopped. Five minutes later it went off again.

I'd never noticed before just how loud fire alarms are.

I wasn't really sleepy anymore so I wandered downstairs to see what was going on.

The alarm system was automated. It had tried to reset itself, but because there was still rainwater dripping through the smoke detector, it had shorted out again. I spent half an hour pushing the "Alarm Silence" button every five seconds while the night manager and another one of the chaperones figured out how to shut the system down.

Later in the night a different chaperone crawled down the corridor on his hands and knees, sniffing at room doors. It's a long story, but pretty darn funny.

Maybe next week. I'm going to bed now.

Okay, let's recap from last week. There I was, one of half a dozen chaperones with 93 teenagers on an educational trip to the Twin Cities. We had checked into a hotel and in the middle of the night had been rousted from bed by a false fire alarm that was not, I repeat NOT, our fault. Everything settled down and people were all back in bed by around 2:30 a.m.

Well, almost everybody.

One of the chaperones was still up and around. The jury is still out about why he was wandering the hotel. It might have been because he was trying to be responsible or it might have been because he snored so loudly his roommate banished him to the hall. The record isn't clear on that, but he was definitely in the hall around 3:00 a.m.

He smelled smoke.

He knew this was something to be concerned

about. The fire department had been very clear
about that. The fire alarm had been disconnected,
everyone else was asleep, so smoke in the hallway
needed to be investigated.

He started down the hallway, sniffing
cautiously. He determined that the smell was
coming from one of the rooms so after a few steps he
dropped to his hands and knees and started sniffing
the bottom of each door. He continued, crawling
down the long hall, sniffing carefully at the crack
under each door.

He told me this story the next morning and
even in the clear light of day every move he made
still made perfect sense, but the visual image I got
of, well, the crawling and sniffing part, was a
little disturbing.

It gets worse. As the smoke smell got stronger
he suddenly realized that this was no ordinary
smoke he smelled. It was more of a pharmaceutical
type smoke. I mean, he smelled burning hemp, but
it wasn't from the back of a rug. This meant there
was still a smoke problem, but one of an entirely
different nature.

He was beginning to wish he hadn't started the
whole crawling and sniffing thing, but he decided
that the only responsible thing to do was finish the
job. He crawled along and soon found a door where
the smoke smell seemed strongest. He pulled out
his room chart and discovered that the suspect
room was occupied by one of the chaperones. He sat
back on his heels and pondered his options. Now he
was really sorry he'd begun the investigation. He
wasn't sure what he was going to do, but he had a
feeling the whole incident wasn't going to look good

in the school board minutes. Suddenly, there was a little stronger waft of smoke and our puzzled hero realized that the smoke was actually coming from the room across the hall. He checked his room chart again and found that the room was not occupied by anyone from our group. He stood up in relief and said the five sweetest words in the English language: "This is not my problem."

He didn't investigate any more mysteries that night.

I don't blame him a bit.

Liars

Why are women better liars than men? We do so much more of it, you'd think the practice would do us good, but it doesn't seem to.

Not only are women better liars, they seem to be able to tell instinctively the correct time to lie and when to just tell the truth. This is a more difficult skill to master than you might think.

For instance, say you are a guy and you're walking through a department store. As you pass the perfume counter, some salesperson accidentally gives you a little spritz with a perfume bottle. You finish your shopping and go home. Your wife walks by you and suddenly stops and sniffs. "Is that perfume I smell?" she says. Now, you have done NOTHING WRONG. Do you tell the truth, or do you make up some lame lie, like, "No, I just stopped by the shop to see how Dick was coming with the new transmission and I helped him lift an engine block up on the stand. He tripped and fell on me, and this is just the smell of a new penetrating oil he's using. It's called 'Lemon Persuasion.'"

Why did you say that? Why couldn't you just tell the truth? Your wife would nod, say, "Oh," and go on her way.

I'll tell you why. You are so used to getting in trouble for things you didn't know were wrong that it's become second nature to you to lie when answering any question, just in case the truth could hurt.

Here's a true story. Before my birthday, I answered the phone one day, and it was our neighbor, who runs a picture framing shop. She asked if my wife was around. When I said no, she said she'd call back. When I saw my wife, I asked her why Marlys had called. She said, "Oh, you know she had that operation, and Bette filled in for her at work, and so she wanted to throw Bette a little party to thank her. I'm supposed to bring cookies."

IT WAS ALL A LIE. She had gotten something framed for me for my birthday; the phone call was to tell her it was ready to be picked up. Not only was it a lie, it was the right lie, at the right time, when nothing but a lie would serve. Now, either she had this lie already prepared and practiced, or else I might as well just blindly believe everything she tells me for the rest of my life, because she is way too good for me.

Richard Nixon was a guy. This is obvious because not only did he lie when he didn't need to, he told a lie everyone could see through, he tried to get his buddies to back him up and take the fall for it, and then he forgot to destroy the evidence. If a woman had been president during Watergate, we'd never have heard a word about it.

City Kids

Our high school does an exchange every year with a big suburban school. It is a good experience all around. We get a vanload of city kids out here on the prairie. A few parents meet at the school and divide them up, so many to pig farms, so many to dairy farms, etc. We call it "Gawk at the Hicks Week." It is always an eye-opening experience for all concerned. We think the kids will be awed by the grandeur of the night sky and the fast-paced life during harvest, when in fact what a lot of them find impressive is that everyone waves to everyone else and there are no stop lights in the entire county. They stay a couple of days, doing cultural stuff like touring the implement dealership, looking at the animals and riding in combines. A few weeks later, our kids go their school and do the same sort of thing. Their hosts show them around the big town, take them to plays and musicals so they can appreciate the broad advantages of living in the cultural center of the state. What seems to impress them the most is that the school they visit is so big the janitors need golf carts to move around in the halls.

In addition to the educational aspects of the exchange, there is also the entertainment factor. We discovered that part of it the very first time we had some kids stay with us. The first evening, one of the young ladies looked at her slightly grubby hands and said in a puzzled tone, "I had no idea there would be so much dirt on a farm."

You know, the problem with being a paid liar is that people are going to think I made this up. I didn't. I couldn't make up stuff this funny. The girl wasn't being rude; all in all, she was very well mannered. It's just that the dirt thing really bothered her.

The next year we had a couple of guys stay with us. My wife enjoyed them a lot, at least partly because even though they didn't know anything about farms, they sure knew how a threshing crew was supposed to eat. If you could avoid the flashing forks, it was a pleasure watching them put the food away. As a farmer, I certainly appreciated the effort they made to cut down on the surplus food problem.

The boys were insatiably curious and I showed them the whole farm from top to bottom. It was dark when I took them to see the combine, which was put away. We keep it in a Quonset that is just barely bigger then the combine. It fits like a cork in a bottle. A very big cork. I hit the switch that opens the bifold door and turned on the lights. One of the guys looked up, saw the combine, threw his arms wide and said, "That is so TOUGH! I like it! What is it?"

You see what I mean? You can't buy entertainment like that.

This year the girls who stayed with us were a joy. They were friendly, curious, asked good questions and were no bother at all.

Took a little bit of the fun out of it, actually.

Norwegians

I've been losing sleep over a fairly serious problem. I hope someone can help me figure it out.

My ancestry is mainly Norwegian. Oh, there's some Welsh, some Irish, and a little bit of other stuff mixed in, but by and large I consider that my bloodlines come from that little country that smells a lot like herring.

My problem is that I don't understand how my ancestors got the reputation that they have. I mean, a common perception of Norwegian-Americans is that we go to church, work hard, and take life seriously.

Okay, the truth. Everyone thinks we're boring. Responsible, hardworking, ethical, but boring. How did that happen? Sure, Norway now is full of throngs of blonde people hanging out, cross-country skiing and wearing sweaters, but a few hundred years ago we were Vikings! I mean, we were the real deal. If countries were plants, Norway would have been poison ivy. If people were food, the Vikings would have been rare prime rib. If armies were sports, the Vikings would have been All-Star Wrestling.

Not only were they tough, they had great names that sounded tough. Names like Eric BloodAxe and Ragnar Hairy Breeches. Would you make Eric BloodAxe the chairman of the church council? I don't think so, although it probably would cut down on whining about tithing and stains on the carpet of the nursery.

Tough isn't all of it, though. They were mean and sneaky. One of their kings, Harold, (THAT'S how tough they were—even the guys named Harold were tough,) was besieging a city with a big wooden stockade around it. He noticed that there were all sorts of birds nesting on the stockade so he had his troops capture the birds, tie strings that were attached to burning bundles of twigs to their legs, and then let them go. The birds flew back to the stockade, set it on fire, and burned the town down.

See? Tough, mean, and sneaky. Sounds like the letterhead for an insurance company law firm, doesn't it. You know, "Tough, Mean, and Sneaky: We're Not on Your Side."

I hope I'm making my point here. The Vikings were not placid folks. You know that song, "London Bridge is Falling Down?" Well, we're the ones who pulled it down! In 1010 a Norwegian, Olaf the Stout (too much lutefisk, no doubt), was attacking London and had his men tie ropes between his ships and London Bridge. Then they rowed away and pulled the bridge down. I'm not sure if they made up the nursery rhyme on the spot or if it came later. I'm hoping it came later. I'm bothered a little bit by the thought of a couple of hairy Vikings holding hands and making an arch while the rest of the crew took turns running through the arch. I'm sure it would have been done in a manly manner, but it does make kind of a goofy mental image. Besides, I'm not at all convinced behavior like that would have aided in the conquest of England.

After the Vikings fizzled out, what happened to us? Sure, the Norwegians were nasty again for a while during World War II, schussing around the mountains blowing up Nazis, but after that they just moved right into boring again.

I don't know how it happened, but I'm not sure I like it. Feared throughout the world and then a 1000 years later the only thing we're famous for is weak coffee and gray food. It makes me want to go burn and pillage something. Oh wait, that's pillage THEN burn, isn't it.

See, we haven't all forgotten our heritage.

Ted

Ted has been having a tough week.

Ted is one of our housecats. It was never part of the plan for him to be a housecat, but his father is our resident tomcat and he beats Ted up every time he goes outside. We had Ted neutered in an attempt to render him harmless in his father's eyes, but it didn't work. In addition to the neutering, Ted has only one eye courtesy of his father, and I'm afraid he's let his figure go to pot. His life has passed beyond tragedy now to humor. You know. "Fat, one-eyed, paranoid, neutered cat. Answers to the name of "Lucky."

Due to his childhood traumas, Ted is a master of the art of looking harmless. Since he looks like a fluffy Siamese, with two extra toes per foot and a body roughly the shape of a bowling ball, it is hard for him to look invisible, but he does his best to look harmless.

His favorite room in the house is the bathroom. I am usually the first person up, and Ted is lonely so he likes to jump in the sink and keep me company while I brush my teeth. Since he is big enough to completely fill up the sink, proper tooth brushing procedures become difficult to follow. It's not easy to spit on a fat, one-eyed cat that is staring up at you and purring. It just isn't what I need to start my day. I usually lock him out of the bathroom, but then he sits outside and hooks the bottom of the door with his paw, trying to pull it open.

Ted is not as agile as a cat really should be. I think the lack of an eye has ruined his depth perception. He has a tendency to leap at things and miss. I watched him jump for the top of a table once. His vertical leap was about six inches short of what was needed so he reached out one desperate foot and grabbed the edge. Unfortunately, what he grabbed was the edge of the tablecloth, and he fell back to the floor with a thump, dragging everything off the table on top of him. If I were a better person, I wouldn't have laughed nearly as hard as I did.

Ted's daddy has come home, after a long absence. Someone shot him through the neck. He has a little hole in the top of his neck and an enormous one on the bottom of his neck. We have to give him antibiotics and smear some salve stuff on the wounds twice a day, so he is living in the house for a while. His daddy may be critically wounded, but he can still beat up Ted, so now Ted has to live outside.

He finds this puzzling and a little frightening. Years of parental abuse have made him wary. He walks slowly everywhere he goes, turning his head from side to side in hopes of seeing with his good eye any potential ambush. He sighs with relief when someone will hold him and guarantee his safety.

I feel sorry for him sometimes. Maybe tomorrow I won't spit on him.

P.S. Two years later Ted and his father are still with us. The old man has gone downhill a long way, holding onto life evidently by using his surplus supply of pure meanness. Ted looks much the same, except he has a chronic ear infection that the vet can't cure. He walks slowly, with his head tipped to one side and he occasionally runs into things. We've changed his name to "Crooked Ted."

It was either that or "Lucky."

Being a Mentor

So there I was, a chaperone on a band and choir trip. I was sitting in a hotel room with a bunch of teenagers, eating some incredibly bad Chinese food. The TV was on and suddenly one of the kids giggled hysterically and said, "Look at that guy! He's bald and he's got a beard! What a freak!"

As many of you know, I have a beard and I'm, well, I'm bald. There was dead silence in the room for about five seconds. Then every eye in the room turned towards me.

I've always thought honesty was an overrated virtue in the young.

It was a shattering experience. One moment, there I am, a mentor and guide to the youth of my community. Well, that may be stretching it a bit, but I did teach them all how to use chopsticks. And the next moment, boom, I'm an object of ridicule based on a couple of unfortunate personal characteristics. Life can be so cruel.

Other than that moment and a few like it, I have to admit I had a pretty good time. Our first stop was in Sioux City to perform at a retirement home. It was supposed to be an outside performance in the courtyard, but by the time we got there the wind had come up so the band had to set up inside. It was kind of cute to see about 57 people turning down their hearing aids simultaneously when the band cut loose.

We left there and headed west across Nebraska in the dark. We drove through Nebraska in the dark coming back too. I suppose that's kind of a win/lose sort of a thing. Nebraska is famous for having the most boring scenery in America, but I never saw any of it.

I'd never been to the Denver area before. I highly recommend it. The scenery is great, and the people are very nice. We pulled into Colorado Springs about 5:30 in the morning and stopped at a Denny's for breakfast. The lone waitress flung her body across the doorway when she saw all 78 teenagers come boiling off the buses, but she relented and let us in when we promised to tip heavily. We could see Pike's Peak out the window of the restaurant as we ate. At least they told us it was Pike's Peak. How would we know if they were telling the truth? We're from western Minnesota. It was a big, cool-looking mountain and if it wasn't really Pike's Peak, don't tell me.

Perhaps the most stressful part of the trip was the next day at Boulder. The plan was to tour the college. When we got there we found out that, due to a logistical foul-up, our tour guides weren't available, so the administration of the college gave each chaperone a map of the campus and told us to take a self-guided tour with small groups of students. Finding my way around places is not my strong point. I've lived in the same house for 21 years and I still forget where the kitchen is sometimes. I took the map and led my group off on our tour. Every now and then one of the students would say, "What's that building?" I would then look at the map and say, "Shut up. Does anyone know the way back to the bus?"

It's not easy being a mentor.

Shooting Myself

Starting at the base of my right thumb I have a three-inch long ridge of shiny pink scar tissue. It ends on the bottom side of my forefinger. A small memento of one of our more memorable social functions, it itches whenever I am about to do something stupid.

Ever since we started farming we celebrated Norwegian Independence Day. The first few years we mainly drank beer and shot rats with a sawed off shotgun. As we grew older our tastes changed and our circle of acquaintances grew wider. The party title changed to Norwegian-Filipino-French Independence Day Celebration and the guest list expanded from two to about one hundred.

Two days before the party I arranged for our local butcher to come out and help me slaughter a pig to roast. When the butcher showed up, it wasn't him, it was his wife. This is not as odd an occurrence in a small town as it would be in a larger place. Most of our local businesses do not have a large on-call staff so there tends to be some cross training among spouses. She brought along her nephew from the city who had evidently shown some interest in the slaughtering process.

I've hunted and killed things all my life and always felt vaguely bad about it. Killing a domestic animal is even worse. It makes me feel like a storm trooper. The reason I do it myself is because I am competent at it. This only seems fair. If you are going to kill something and eat it, the least you can do is give it a quick, painless death.

If you make an imaginary X between the ears and the eyes of most animals, a shot about an inch above the center of the X will drop them as if they have just noticed gravity. I drew the X with my eyes and put the bullet right where I wanted to. Nothing happened. There was a small blue hole in the middle of the hog's forehead, but the animal still stood there. To this day I don't know what happened. As I took aim again the pig turned to run away. I grabbed hold of its ear to hold the head in place. Just as I pulled the trigger the pig jerked its head and I shot myself in the hand.

At this point in the story I always begin to blush. The problem is that there is no way to put myself in a favorable light. If you are in a car accident, for instance, there is almost always a way to tell the story so it appears that you are a helpless victim. When you pick up a rifle, take careful aim, and shoot yourself in the hand, it is difficult to look like anything other than a complete buffoon.

I looked at my hand and saw a bluish-black groove about a half-inch deep starting to fill with blood. It had the look of something that couldn't be fixed with a Band-Aid. The pig did fall.

As I walked toward the house I was trying to think of a tactful way to tell my wife that I had shot myself. The butcher and her nephew trailed along behind me, no doubt trying to stay out of my line of fire. From past experience I knew that bloodstains were hard to clean up off our floor so I stayed outside. I shouted to my wife in a tactful manner that I had shot myself and needed some medical attention. I looked down and saw one of our cats sitting next to me licking my blood off the lawn. To this day I take great pride in the fact that I did not kick it.

My wife had some trouble communicating with our doctor, as he kept breaking up in giggles every time she tried to explain what I had done. He finally settled down enough to agree to meet me at the clinic. My wife stayed home to help finish the butchering, and I drove off with the nephew riding shotgun in case I began to drive as well as I aimed. He sat as far away as possible, no doubt afraid that stupidity was contagious. My hand was starting to hurt and it was leaking red through the bath towel wrapped around it. The ride was a bit awkward. It is hard to talk to a strange 14 year old who has just seen you do something incredibly dumb. You know the stilted conversations you have when you're taking the baby-sitter home? You say stuff like, "So, what grade are you in?" and get monosyllabic answers in return. This was worse, a lot worse.

Our doctor met me at the door of the clinic. He tried his best to convince me that he had seen lots of people do things as stupid as this, although when pressed he couldn't come up with any examples except the Maginot Line and the designated hitter in baseball.

The hand was really starting to hurt, so he gave me a wonderful injection. Two minutes after the needle hit my arm it was as if a big red wave washed over me and swept all my troubles away. There have been times since then when it has been a temptation to shoot myself again if it would guarantee me another shot like that one.

I probably would not have been so relaxed if I had known what was going on at home. Unbeknownst to me, my wife was calling the guest list for our party to tell them that it had to be postponed for a week. I knew that this wasn't the sort of thing that I could keep secret, but I really hadn't counted on being a known idiot so quickly.

My sister-in-law drove me home, because I was still drifting in the arms of whatever was in my bloodstream. After a while the shot wore off, and I contemplated a long sleepless night. I decided to lie on the couch and hope something interesting came on the late show. My wife kissed me on my bald spot and headed upstairs. It hadn't really been a banner day from her point of view either. I heard her footsteps on the stairs, then heard the light switch click on. Then, I heard her scream. For some completely inexplicable reason, other than to fulfill the adage that some days are better than others, the wiring in our hall light shorted out. Sparks started to drip from the light fixture, followed by a ball of flame, followed by darkness.

My wife is a wonderful woman in every respect, except she is less than 5'2" and cannot reach any light in the house, even standing on a chair. She came and got me up, helped me up on a chair, and braced herself against my knee so I wouldn't blow over. I stripped charred wires and capped them while holding a flashlight in my teeth.

If you ever hire an electrician and he shows up on your doorstep with a gunshot wound and an injection of morphine, don't let him in. Trust me, he won't do a very good job.

I can't remember what was on the late show. I remember I didn't enjoy it.

Cruise

A while back my son called me and asked if I wanted to go on a cruise with him. I asked if I could get a deck chair by the pool. He said there was no pool, there were no deck chairs. He thought with luck he'd be able to find me a non-greasy piece of steel to squat on.

I thought it sounded great.

You have to understand, I don't get out much.

My son's unit was on its way back from Kuwait and if I was willing to pay the government the cost of transporting me, I could travel back on the ship with him from Hawaii to San Diego. I leapt at the opportunity. I suffered a few pangs of guilt over leaving my wife and daughters in Minnesota in February while I jetted off to Hawaii, but I'm strong; I got over it.

My son met me at the airport and we checked in on his ship, the single largest moving object I've ever seen. I've planted fields smaller than that ship. It was all gray steel, helicopters, fighter planes, and various dangerous looking objects. Just being near it boosted my testosterone level . We looked around the ship for a while but because I was still on Minnesota time, I went to bed pretty early. I was sleeping in a bunk 18 inches wide, stacked four high, with a two-foot alley between the rows. The last time I'd been in a bed that small I was trying to get a baby to fall asleep in his crib.

Twenty-four guys lived in an area about the size of my living room. Twenty-three of those guys were just straggling back from shore leave. This was not a restful environment.

The next morning was painful. Not only did I not get any sleep, it was also a little humiliating. There were about 1700 Marines on the ship. By and large they are young men between 19 and 22, in the best physical shape you can imagine. As they were getting ready for their day, they were dressed mainly in towels, tattoos and muscles. In the middle of these fine specimens were about 200 fat old men, myself included. I saw one guy on his way to the shower who was putting so much effort into holding his stomach in that his arms stuck out to the sides like a roast chicken.

There was one very sweet moment though. My son was responsible for me and well, to be honest, I am a slob. In order to keep from getting chewed out for my sloppy bunk he had to make my bed for me every morning. I accepted his services in honor of parents everywhere.

We left dock, and I did not get seasick. I was congratulating myself on my Viking ancestors when we left the harbor and entered the actual ocean. I took a little Dramamine.

After the Dramamine kicked in we wandered down to get some breakfast.

Over the years I've heard a lot of guys complaining about the food they got in the service. I've also read newspaper articles telling about how much money the government spends on food for people in the military. I think I've figured out the problem.

Every meal on that ship had food in it that at one time was really, really, good. I didn't actually get to taste much of it, but you could clearly see the quality, or former quality, of the ingredients.

The problem is that when you start feeding a couple of thousand people, some things get cold, some get tough, and some things get burned. With luck, you get a terrific meal. With bad luck, everything you eat is cold, tough, and burned.

The next few days are a blur. I got to see jets dropping bombs, guys leaping out of helicopters, and all sorts of other nifty demonstrations. I found out I have a lot more in common with enlisted men than with officers. I found out I could almost sleep while holding myself in bed to keep from rolling out, and I got to spend more time with my son than I have since he was two.

All in all, it was just about the most fun I've ever had.

Chick Household

I live in a totally chick household. It wasn't always this way. When our son was young, men outnumbered women here two to one. Then a couple daughters came along, he grew up and joined the Marine Corps, and now here I am, outnumbered three to one.

Most days I don't even notice it, but there are times. For instance, we are watching football and there is some particularly vicious hit, with some poor slob smeared across the field like a windshield bug. I notice if I am watching with one of my womenfolk, they'll say something like, " Oh, my Lord! Why did he hit him so hard!"

Now, if my son were home, we'd give each other high fives and say, "Yeah! Good hit, Bubba! Look at that, intestines smeared all over his helmet." Most women don't seem to appreciate the finer points of sports.

It's not all bad, of course. Being surrounded by women does seem to bring out the finer points of living. Napkins, for instance. They're not an implement I use a lot when I'm alone. I've always thought that's why shirttails were invented. My wife is kind of a stickler for them, though. Why just the other day she looked at me and said, quietly, "Do you have a napkin?"

I thought it was a stupid question. Of course I had a napkin. I smiled and held it up to show to her, then went on eating and at the same time continued telling her a fascinating story. She started making odd gestures with her little finger at the side of her mouth. I thought it looked strange, but hey, I've been married a long time; you've got to learn to cut someone a little slack. Finally, right when I had reached the best part of the story she interrupted me and said, "You have a lump of mayonnaise the size of Connecticut in your beard."

She can be so rude sometimes.

That's another strange thing about women. They don't like it when the sink is full of dirty dishes, but they insist on using all sorts of plates and eating utensils on a regular basis. One way or the other, ladies. Make up your mind.

I am usually alone for lunch, and I can have a perfectly good meal and dirty only one dish. Sometimes, if I just have a sandwich, I can lick the knife clean that I used to butter the bread and it's a zero utensil meal. My hero is a guy I know who used to heat up Dinty Moore stew without taking it out of the can. He'd eat it with chopsticks, lick off the chopsticks and throw away the can. What a man!

We don't need to go into the whole toilet seat up and down thing. Just a little better observation on the part of the womenfolk and it wouldn't be a problem.

Did you know that a lot of women change their socks *every day*?

Children

The other day I was talking to a guy who has two children. He was telling me that his biggest concern is that when his children are about thirty years old they will come to him one at a time. The first one will tell him, "Dad, I really appreciate how hard you worked to make enough money to send me to college, but I think you should know that you missing all those t-ball games has scarred me for life." Then the other kid will come to him and say, "Dad, I do thank you for the effort you made to attend as many of my school plays as you did, but if you would have devoted more time to your career, you could have made enough money to send me to Harvard. The lack of a good education has ruined my life."

It isn't so much the fact that he pretty much accepts that his children will blame him for wrecking their future. *What concerns him is that they will blame him no matter what he does.* If they both have the same complaint about him, it means that with the best intentions he just made the wrong decision. Everyone knows how that feels. You are presented with a situation, you worry about it, ask other people what they would do, consult with your spouse, come up with a united plan of attack, and then have it all come crashing down around your head. When that happens, all you can do is shrug your shoulders and say, "Oh well, I really thought it was the right thing to do."

On the other hand, with my friend's scenario, we're pretty much doomed right from the start and it is best we know it so we can avoid any kind of overconfidence.

I know exactly how he feels. I had no idea, absolutely none, what a baffling job parenthood was going to be. It sounds fairly simple. You have babies, you change diapers and shove bottles in their mouths until they are trained and can cook for themselves. When the kids are about five or six you turn them over to the school system and it takes over. At age 18 the school system gives you back well-prepared young people and you have a big party and send them out into the world. Then you turn their room into a den and start spending winters in Arizona. After a while you get grandchildren and then all you have to do is give them too much chocolate and chase them around the house making monster sounds right before they go home to go to bed. In between, you play catch with the kid and if it's a girl you threaten any boys that come to your house.

If any of you out there are considering parenthood, I don't want to discourage you, but it's a lot more complicated than that.

It seems like a fairly simple concept. No one ever told me about all the problems you can't solve, let alone the problems that you don't even understand.

No one ever told me that you worry about your kids forever and even when they are happy the experienced parent can find the seeds of disaster in any triumph.

I'm already dreading what they are going to say to me when they're 30.

Class Reunions

I was talking to a young woman today who is anticipating her ten-year class reunion. I can't say eagerly anticipating. I can't say as I blame her. Despite having been out of high school for almost 25 years, I've been to only one class reunion. As I remember, I had a wonderful time, but I certainly didn't think I was going to.

She is already uneasy, because the organizers want all class members to include a little biographical sketch that will be made into a booklet for each person. She's been out of high school for ten years. She's gone to college, and she's gotten a job. These are worthy accomplishments, but not really, you know, fascinating reading. I had several suggestions for her.

"Dear classmates: I have had an active and interesting ten years. Unfortunately, because I am now enrolled in the Federal Witness Protection Program and am currently undergoing plastic surgery in Barcelona, I will be unable to attend this year's reunion or ever talk to any of you again the rest of my life. I have many wonderful stories I would just love to share, but if I told you I would have to kill you. Best wishes to all."

"Dear classmates: As many of you know, I entered Harvard immediately after graduation from high school. I am pleased to announce that just last month I completed my college education with master's degrees in both Comparative French Literature and Sixteenth Century Philosophy. Despite advice from people who told me the job market was limited in those areas, I am thrilled to be using my education to the fullest as the assistant night manager of a Quickie Stop in Des Moines. Meeting my $2000 per month school loan payment is a bit of a struggle, but I have been assured by management that as soon as my mopping skills are a bit more polished, I am in line for a $.13 per hour raise."

"Dear classmates: I am so eager to meet all of you again and share my enlightenment. I have shed the false teachings of my youth and have been reborn into the congregation of The One Great Wookie. Because I am so fond of all of you, I am more than willing to spend as much time as is needed to convince each and every one of you of the necessity of abandoning your earthly desires for the purity of life within the embrace of Wookiedom."

"Dear classmates: I am pleased that I have been invited to attend our class reunion even though I did not actually graduate with our class, due to that unfortunate incident involving stolen explosives and gun running from South America. (I was framed.) It looks like I will be out on parole in time for the reunion, and I have had ten long years to think about who was nice to me in high school AND who wasn't. I am very eager to see you all. I have some real surprises in store for you!"

You see? Class reunions don't have to be boring. If nothing else, use one of these letters and there should be plenty of room at your table.

Graduation

No one has ever asked me to speak at a graduation ceremony, but if someone ever does, I have a speech ready.

It was no bother. Over the years I've prepared a lot of speeches that I'll probably never get a chance to deliver. My acceptance speech for the Nobel Peace Prize is a doozy. And you know that award People Magazine gives out every year, the one for the Sexiest Man Alive? I don't want to go into details here, but if the phone ever rings and the caller is People Magazine, I'm prepared to be modest, charming, and, of course, sexy.

Anyway, because I know a number of young people who are graduating this year I thought I'd share a few thoughts with them.

Let me start by saying, "congratulations." Thanks to orthodontia, Head Start, better nutrition, and the stock market, as a group you are the prettiest, smartest, tallest, and richest group of young people in American history. The day you graduate people telling you that you are wonderful will surround you. Let them. You are.

The other thing that will happen today is that people will give you advice. Here is mine.

First of all, learn how to get by. "Getting by" is an ancient and honorable profession. An example would be cashing your paycheck, paying the rent, utilities, etc., and finding you only have $10 to live on until the end of the month. In this situation you have two choices. You can either eat all your meals in restaurants that take credit cards and go shopping to take your mind off your money troubles or you can live on tomato soup and peanut butter until payday rolls around. The first choice is called "stupidity" and the second one is called "getting by." Most of you will live 50 or 60 more years. The first 50 years of this century saw two world wars and the Great Depression. There's no reason to think the first 50 years of the next century won't be just as interesting. At some point in your life, knowing how to get by will be a valuable tool.

Second, take risks. I'm not talking about being stupid. The Guinness Book of World Records is already plenty thick enough. There's no need to try anything tricky with bungee cords or speeding cars. By taking risks I mean get out there in the world and look around. Go places you've never been, eat food you've never tried, talk to people you've never met. Experience is a great teacher, so try to have a lifetime of it.

Third, money isn't all that important. I know, I may be paddling upstream alone here, but the truth is, money doesn't buy happiness. There are a lot of neat things that you can do if you have money, but that's all it is, just a tool. It shouldn't be a goal in itself. Try to find a job that lets you walk out of the house smiling on Mondays. There are some out there, it's just that they don't usually pay very well.

There are a few of you who are leaping about, happy in the knowledge that your education is finished, so I'll try to break this gently. Graduating from high school isn't that big a deal. The only real purpose of your first twelve years of education was to teach you to read and how to share toys at recess. Oh sure, there's a little math and personal hygiene thrown in, but the bottom line is you have a lot to learn. Your real education starts tomorrow, when you come down the stairs and your folks have a menu, with prices, next to your plate at the breakfast table.

But that's tomorrow. Today, have a great time. Go to the reception after graduation. Stand straight, shake hands, keep smiling. Oh, and let Aunt Ruth kiss you on the cheek. She gave you a nice card and it's not her fault she has whiskers.

After it's all over get a good night's sleep. There's a big, wonderful world out there, full of miracles and goofy people and in 20 or 30 years, you'll be running it.

You have a lot to do.

Rats

I don't like rats. I don't want them on my farm or in my barns. Since my wife made it clear that the first time she saw a rat in the house would be the last time she set foot in the house, I certainly don't want rats there. Rats are filthy and spread disease. They are destructive, wrecking buildings by chewing holes in them and spoiling grain meant for a hungry world. Plus, let's face it. They're ugly. Sometimes pet stores offer white rats for sale. White rats are even less appealing than regular rats. I think maybe it's because of the red eyes. Rats with red eyes look like they should be groupies for a rock band called Sons of Satan.

My dislike of rats extends to the other members of the rat family. Namely: gerbils, hamsters, and guinea pigs. Sure, you may say they are far different than rats. I disagree. They're just small rats, tailless rats, and hairy rats as far as I'm concerned.

Now, don't get offended and stop me on the street to tell me how your pet hamster Bruno saved the lives of the family one night when the furnace overheated and started the drapes on fire. You won't convince me that Bruno went from bedroom to bedroom, squeaking and nipping at everyone's toes. I just won't believe you. In that situation, what a rat would do is leap out of a window to safety and then sharpen a stick to roast marshmallows while it watched the house burn.

I hope I've established the fact that I really don't care much for rats. The funny thing is, I know a guy who likes rats even less than I do and he has one for a house pet. Let me explain.

This guy has a child. The child was in a class in which the students studied a couple of white rats as a class project. Of course, the study came to a close after a while, probably because you can only spend so much time telling your class, "Look children, a rat. Isn't it ugly?" The problem was what to do with the rats at the end of the study. The solution was to have a lottery, and the sucker, I mean the winning child, would get to take a rat home to live forever and ever. My friend found out about this plan when his child came home with a permission slip to enter the rat lottery. His child really wanted that rat. Who knows why? Kids can be weird. The dad thought about it for a while, as his child leapt up and down in front of him yelling, "Please, please, please, Daddy!" What he decided was, why not? There were 23 kids in the class and only *two* rats. That meant his kid had a better than 90 percent chance of coming home ratless. All Dad had to do was give permission. His child wouldn't hate him, and when he found out that he didn't win the rat, they would go out to Dairy Queen to mourn their loss. I would have done the same thing.

Well, you guessed it. They won the rat. The dad couldn't believe his bad luck. Some time later he met the teacher and asked how many kids had entered the lottery to win one of the two rats.

"Two," she said.

Dinnertime

I heard the saddest story.

Well, it wasn't sad the way the guy told it, but I bet it felt tragic at the time. Here it is.

My friend, who needs to remain nameless because he worked on a project involving government stupidity and was foolish enough to tell them with some detail how stupid they were, does bookkeeping for farmers. Actually, he does a lot more than that, but a major component of his job is helping farmers set up and run computerized accounting systems.

As part of his job, he had the opportunity to apply for a government-sponsored, short-term project and was accepted.

The task he was assigned was to go to one of the former provinces of the Soviet Union, "something, something stahn" and teach their farmers computerized accounting procedures. This seemed to be right up his alley work wise and would give him an interesting line on his resume, not to mention a potential for some good stories.

If only he'd known.

He packed up some clothes and his laptop computer and caught a plane for the wilds of "something, something stahn."

Actually, it was probably more than one plane. I think it was a couple of different trains, a bus, and maybe an oxcart. He arrived at his destination tired and jet lagged, but ready to work.

Unfortunately, he couldn't.

It seems that his potential clients weren't quite ready to be introduced to the wonders of computerized farm accounting procedures. They were still nomads, following their herds around the steppes. Not only were there no computers, they didn't have electricity and were a little short on pencils too. My friend was a little baffled by this, but then realized, hey, this is the former Soviet Union, there's nobody alive here who knows how to turn a profit. He decided he could tell them stuff like "buy low and sell high" and imagined them all slapping their foreheads in amazement. He worked in a few nuances like knowing how much it cost to produce a sheep and why it's important to sell the sheep for more than that. Life was pretty good until a new problem reared its ugly head.

Literally.

As my friend traveled from place to place, he was treated as somewhat of a celebrity. Being a celebrity had its downside, because in that culture an honored guest is treated to a meal of boiled sheep's head, and part of the honor is that the guest gets to eat the sheep's eyes.

No, I'm not lying.

It gets worse.

You see, my friend didn't just work with one group of nomads. His job was to travel from group to group. And at EVERY STOP he was the honored guest.

Now, there's a limit to the number of boiled sheep's eyes your average American can eat. He'd made it through the first meal by just repeating to himself that the honor of the U.S.A. was at stake, then he'd closed his eyes and thought of boiled eggs and overripe plums.

That only worked once.

I'm still proud of him for his solution. Good old American ingenuity at work. At his next stop, when he was told there would be a special banquet that night to celebrate his status as an honored guest, he waved his arms and said, in an emotional voice, "No, that's impossible, because you have made me so welcome I no longer feel like a stranger, but like a member of the family, so for our meal tonight, I want to eat nothing special."

Everyone got all teary-eyed, hugged him and then settled down to a nice supper of rice and fried goat.

No eyes.

At the end of the day, of course, I'm just a guy. A father, a husband, and a farmer. Despite being a chubby, bald, pig farmer, which puts me outside of the mainstream of American life, I know that my world isn't that much different than yours. I know that, because I hear from people all the time, telling me that the story I told in my column last week was just like something that had happened to them. Then they tell me their story, and it's usually better than mine.

We are all in this together. I hope you've enjoyed my stories, and I hope our paths cross some day so you can have a chance to tell me some of yours.

What Planet

A reporter called the other day and wanted to interview me about how to keep a sense of humor during the current farm crisis. His first question was, "How are you doing?"

I said, "Well, it's spring, the birds are singing and the sun is shining. Life is good."

There was a long pause: then he said, "What planet do you live on?"

I live on this one, most of the time anyway.

Trust me. No one, and I mean NO ONE, needs to tell me how frustrating and discouraging the current farming situation is. People I've known my whole life are leaving the area and people I cherish are getting out of the business of agriculture. On Monday I will ship the last of my sows off to market. I've lost just too much money to keep on raising hogs. With all that, it is easy to get down and hard to come back up again.

There is something I think about that helps, most of the time.

We live in a country founded by people who woke up one morning, looked around, and said, "I can do better than this." They picked up, lock, stock, and barrel, and headed to a new land and a new life, leaving all that was familiar and comfortable behind. Sometimes I feel like my family has been here for a long time. My great-grandparents homesteaded my farm about 120 years ago. What I usually forget is that they came from a place where their family had lived for a 1000 years, maybe 2000. Adolph and Marie left all that in an effort to find a better life for the family they hoped to start. You know what? They were right. It wasn't easy, but they did make a better life for themselves and their descendants.

Now, my point here is this: I love this little corner of the world where I live. It's easy to make fun of it, with its heat and cold, storms and droughts, lack of scenery and occasionally narrow-minded people. In spite of all that, it is still the place I chose to live. But it isn't *why* I live. I live for my family, and it's important to remember that. You shouldn't invest too much of yourself in a place. Save your commitments for people.

This thing we're going through right now in agriculture is pretty bad. Some people are going to lose their farms and others are going to lose their jobs. The schools are going to get smaller, and there are going to be fewer people to do the work of the community. It's nothing I want to see happen, but there are a lot of things in this world of which I disapprove.

I may be wrong here. Lord knows, I've been wrong about a lot of things. It could be that we are on the edge of a bright new day in rural America. The phrase, "It's always darkest before the dawn," has been true quite a few times.

On the other hand, if things do get worse and some of us are forced to wake up, look around, and say, "This isn't working. I can do better than this," don't worry about it.

The place doesn't matter. The people do. Do what's right for your family.

The End